THE IMPATIENT GOURMET

208 Delicious and Exciting Recipes That Are
Ready to Serve in 30 Minutes or Less

Plus

20 Everyday Dinner Menus,
10 Formal Dinner Menus, and
24 Special-Event Menus

Lillian Beery Willis and Margaret Evans Jeffcoat

Line Drawings by Judith Brooks

CONTENTS

DEDICATION

To our husbands, David and Sid,
    who put up with and put on much;
To David, William, and Sam and
    Karen, Kristin, and Jeff,
    our children, who endured timing and
    testing because of the tasting; and
To all our friends who constantly asked,
    "How's the cookbook coming?"

FOREWORD

Gourmet cooking doesn't have to be time-consuming, mysterious, serious, or expensive. Cooking can be simple and fun. Hence this book with 208 enticing recipes that can be prepared and served in 30 minutes or less—delicious, proven recipes that give both inspiration and instruction for a fast dinner or a feast; that are not loaded with hidden steps and exotic ingredients; that are not just more fascinating ways to cook a hot dog. The vast majority of our recipes would delight you in any top gourmet restaurant and would intrigue you even if speed were not a factor. Those that are not supreme *haute cuisine* are truly appealing and tasty.

The recipes themselves are straightforward, clear, and concise. We've spelled out all ingredients and utensils at the beginning of each—ingredients easily found in the supermarket and utensils readily available in the kitchen of the average cook. And we've also given cooking instructions in great detail. Purists might cringe at some of our shortcuts, but we believe the enjoyable ends justify the means.

To make each recipe work smoothly in the stated time span, you must read through the recipe first and organize all the ingredients and utensils . . . good habits for any cook. You will find that some recipes may require a little practice; but all times have been proven accurate by a variety of cooks on a variety of equipment over the past few years.

Most of the recipes are planned to serve two adults. This fits the life-style of many: students, working people, newlyweds, commuting wives or husbands, and couples whose children are either off at school or off on their own. The twosome quantities are also easy to halve or expand.

There are, however, some exceptions to this rule: hors d'œuvre are usually reserved for parties, so most of those recipes are geared to serve more than two; and for convenience it's easier to make salad dressings and some soups and desserts in quantity.

We have two menu sections—both of which are highly imaginative: with a touch of classic French, a touch of Swiss, a touch of the Deep South, a touch of Mother, and a touch of us. We have created highly original recipes or found ways to shortcut or improve old favorites.

Our Everyday Dinner section gives you four five-day weeks of complete dinners (including dessert!), which you can prepare and cook in 30 minutes. You will be amazed at what you can actually do in that time.

Our Party menu section is *not* restricted to the 30-minute requirement, although many of the supper or brunch menus could easily fit the time standard. No one could expect to complete an intriguing five-course dinner for eight in half an hour. In this party section, our aim was to show how aptly most of our recipes provide exciting dining with new and interesting combinations that please both the palate and the eye. You will also discover how well and easily you can entertain on much less than you might have expected, since our recipes make the most of all ingredients by stretching meat portions, using fresh herbs and vegetables where practical, and taking advantage of delicious little-used vegetables that don't deserve neglect when they are prepared with a little imagination and skill.

In short, we've provided brief, easy-to-understand, delicious recipes that make the most of time, money, effort, and imagination. We and our families, friends, and dinner guests have enjoyed every mouthful; we hope you will, too.

HORS D'OEUVRE
and
APPETIZERS

HORS D'ŒUVRE

See also Index for:

Nutty Little Meatballs
Cheese Fondue
Shrimp Fondue

APPETIZERS

See also Index for:

Avocado with Crunchy Stuffing
Endive Rémoulade
Marinated Mushroom Salad
Pasta Salad
Peggy's Caesar Salad
Sweet-and-Sour Wilted Salad
Almond Fettucini
Asparagus-Cheese Puff
Cheese Rarebit
Crustless Quiche au Fromage Varié
Curried Crab Pie
Fried Mozzarella
Ham-and-Cheese Sandwiches
Scallops à la Newburg
Shrimp Sauté

BLUE ENDIVE

An impressive and unique hors d'œuvre or first course for two. Leftover cheese mixture is also good as a salad dressing when thinned with a little mayonnaise.

INGREDIENTS	UTENSILS
1/2 c. whipping cream	1-qt. measuring pitcher
1/3 c. crumbled blue or Roquefort	measuring cup
cheese	fork
2 firm endive	electric mixer
	paring knife
	plastic wrap
	1 paper towel
	1 serving plate

Measure cream in large pitcher. Crumble cheese with fork and add to cream. Beat until smooth and of the consistency of whipped cream. Cover and refrigerate until served.

Just before serving, spoon cheese mixture onto the center of the serving plate. Rinse whole endive (breaking off any brown outer leaves) and dry. Slice 1/2″ off each bottom and discard. Arrange leaves from each endive around cheese mixture like spokes on a wheel. Serve immediately.

Time: 5 minutes

SHRIMP AND ENDIVE REMOULADE

An impressive presentation and a delicious beginning to any meal.

INGREDIENTS	UTENSILS
8 large shrimp	paper towel
1 medium endive	plastic wrap
1 qt. hot water	2-qt. pot
1 tsp. salt	cutting board
4 ripe olives	paring knife
1/2 c. rémoulade sauce	colander or
(see Index)	large strainer
	serving spoon
	2 salad plates

Bring water and salt to boil over high heat. Meanwhile, wash shrimp and remove shells with fingers. Leave tails intact. Make a shallow cut lengthwise down back of each shrimp; wash out sand vein. Add shrimp to boiling water. Return to boil. Remove from heat and drain. Wrap shrimp in plastic wrap and place in freezer for 15 minutes.

Wipe endive with damp towel. Cut the top 2 inches off the endive and reserve. Slice remaining endive into 1/2" pieces, discarding very bottom. Slice olives.

Place 1/4-cup remoulade sauce on each salad plate. Mound half of the 1/2" endive slices in the center of each plate. Top with olive slices. Alternating shrimp and 2" endive slices, make a pinwheel around the edge of the mound. Serve immediately.

Time: 25-30 minutes
Serves: 2

ARTICHOKE DIP

A simple, savory dip for vegetables or crackers. For a treat to the eye and palate, serve in a scooped-out cabbage surrounded by fresh snow peas.

INGREDIENTS	UTENSILS
1 6-oz. jar marinated artichoke hearts, undrained	blender or food processor
4 oz. cream cheese	rubber spatula
1 pt. sour cream	medium bowl with cover

Blend artichoke hearts and cream cheese until smooth. Remove to bowl and fold in sour cream. Cover and refrigerate until ready to serve.

Time: 3 minutes
Makes: approximately 3 cups

AVOCADO DIP

This is a great dip for all fresh vegetables. Can be made a day in advance.

INGREDIENTS	UTENSILS
1/2 avocado, peeled and sliced	blender or food processor
1/2 c. Hellmann's mayonnaise	measuring spoons
1/2 tsp. salt	paring knife
1/4 tsp. black pepper	rubber spatula
1/8 tsp. garlic powder	cutting board
large sprig fresh parsley	
1 green onion, chopped coarsely	
2 tsp. lemon juice	
1 tbsp. ketchup	

Measure mayonnaise in blender. Prepare avocado and onion and add with all other ingredients to blender. Cover and blend 30-60 seconds or until smooth. Cover and refrigerate until ready to serve.

Time: 3-5 minutes
Makes: 3/4-1 cup

4

BLACK BEAN DIP

No one will ever guess this dip is made from a can of soup. Great when first made, it's even better when given 24 hours for the flavors to intensify.

INGREDIENTS
1 11-oz. can Campbell's
   Black Bean Soup
1/4 tsp. cayenne pepper
2 tsp. onion powder
1 tbsp. chili powder
   (or more, to taste)
4 tsp. lemon juice
2 tbsp. sour cream

UTENSILS
1-pt. plastic container
   with lid
measuring spoons
fork
rubber spatula
serving dish
can opener

Mix all ingredients with fork in plastic container until thoroughly blended and smooth. Cover and refrigerate until ready to serve. Serve with some kind of crisp, light cracker (such as Wheat Thins).

Time: 3 minutes
Makes: approximately 1½ cups

CURRY COCKTAIL DIP

Almost everyone has a favorite curry dip; but ours is the simplest and the best. It's even better made a day in advance so the flavors can intensify.

INGREDIENTS
1 c. Hellmann's mayonnaise
1 tsp. curry powder
1 tsp. minced, dried onion
1 tsp. dried parsley
1 tsp. lemon juice

UTENSILS
2-c. measuring jar with
   lid
measuring spoons
fork

Combine all ingredients in jar. Blend with fork, cover, and refrigerate. Serve with raw cauliflower, string beans, radishes, carrots, celery, cherry tomatoes, olives, pickled ears of corn, sliced white turnip, or sugar snap pea pods.

Time: 2-3 minutes
Makes: approximately 1 cup

CURRIED CRAB SPREAD

So fantastic that people who usually don't like curry will adore this. Freezes well.

INGREDIENTS
1 8-oz. package cream cheese at
   room temperature
1 6-oz. package frozen crab meat,
   thawed, with excess liquid
   squeezed from bag
1½ tsp. curry powder
1/2 tsp. white pepper
1½ tsp. salt
5 tsp. lemon juice
1/4 c. chopped walnuts

UTENSILS
medium bowl
measuring spoons
fork
rubber spatula
ovenproof serving dish
nut choppper or food
   processor

Preheat oven to 350°.
   Chop nuts. Thoroughly mix all ingredients in bowl with fork. Transfer crab mixture to baking dish and bake for 20 minutes. Serve with crisp crackers, endive or artichoke leaves, or celery stalks. Leftover is easily reheated. Add 5 minutes to cooking time if mixture has been frozen.

Time: preparation: 5 minutes
        baking: 20 minutes
Makes: approximately 1½ cups

SHRIMP PATE

An easy dish with snappy flavor. Serve with cucumber rounds, mild crackers (such as Bremner Wafers), or dark bread. Can be made several days in advance.

INGREDIENTS
1 4-oz. can tiny shrimp
1/8 tsp. garlic powder
1/4 tsp. salt
1/2 tsp. dried dill weed
   (or more, to taste)
1 tbsp. Dijon mustard
2 tbsp. butter
1 tbsp. fresh parsley, minced

UTENSILS
food processor or
   blender
measuring spoons
rubber spatula
can opener
paring knife
cutting board

Combine all ingredients but parsley in food processor. Blend. Put into small serving dish, a large seashell, or hollowed green pepper. Mince parsley. Sprinkle parsley on top of shrimp mixture and serve.

Time: 3-5 minutes
Makes: approximately 3/4 cup

ONION CHEESE SPREAD

This is also delicious on hot English muffins for a lunch or snack. Can be made several days in advance. Freezes well.

INGREDIENTS
1/2 envelope Lipton's onion soup
   mix
1 8-oz. package cream cheese at
   room temperature
2 oz. Gruyère cheese, grated

UTENSILS
fork
mixing spoon
cheese grater
1-pt. plastic container
   with lid

Grate Gruyère cheese into plastic container and spoon in the soup mix. Add cream cheese and mix thoroughly with fork. Cover and refrigerate until ready to serve. Serve with crackers (such as Triscuits), celery, or endive.

Time: 3-5 minutes
Makes: approximately 1 cup

PUFFED CHEESE SPREAD

Serve this delicious, hot, puffy spread with mild crackers (such as Wheat Thins), carrot or celery sticks, or slices of apple with the peel left on. Remember to serve the apple immediately after cutting, or the slices will discolor. If you don't wish to serve apple slices, add one tablespoon of grated apple to the cheese mixture before cooking for a different taste.

INGREDIENTS
2 tbsp. chopped walnuts
2 tbsp. grated onions
3/4 c. sharp Cheddar cheese,
   shredded
1/3 c. Hellmann's mayonnaise
1/8 tsp. salt
1/8 tsp. dry mustard
1/8 tsp. Worcestershire sauce

UTENSILS
large bowl
measuring spoons
measuring cup
food processor or
   blender and grater
paring knife
fork
ovenproof serving dish

Preheat oven to 350°.
   Chop nuts, grate onion, and shred cheese with food processor—adding each to large bowl as it is prepared. Add mayonnaise, salt, mustard, and Worcestershire sauce to bowl. Stir well with fork and transfer mixture to baking dish. Pat flat and cook for 20 minutes. Serve immediately.

Time: preparation: 5 minutes
        cooking: 20 minutes
Makes: 1 cup

CHEDDAR CHEESE BALL

A most unusual and pretty interpretation of a familiar favorite. Can be made several days in advance. Freezes well.

INGREDIENTS
1/2 c. grated Cheddar cheese
  (about 4 oz.)
1 8-oz. package cream cheese
  at room temperature
1 4½-oz. can chopped ripe olives
2 tbsp. horseradish
1/8 tsp. cayenne pepper
  (or more, to taste)
1/8 tsp. salt
1 c. chopped pecans or walnuts

UTENSILS
large bowl
measuring cup
measuring spoons
electric mixer
rubber spatula
cheese grater
nut chopper or blender
  or food processor
15" piece waxed paper

Grate Cheddar cheese into bowl. Add all other ingredients except nuts and blend with electric mixer. Chop nuts. Form mixture into ball, and roll in nuts on waxed paper. Fold waxed paper around ball and refrigerate until ready to serve with crackers.

Time: 10 minutes

BEEF BALL

This is also excellent as a spread for sandwiches or as a stuffing for celery or cherry tomatoes. Can be made a day in advance. Freezes well.

INGREDIENTS
1 3-oz. package of smoked, sliced,
  pressed, cooked beef
1 3-oz. package of cream cheese
  at room temperature
1 tsp. Worcestershire sauce
1/4 tsp. pepper
2 tbsp. sour cream
1/2 c. fresh parsley, minced

UTENSILS
blender or
  food processor
paring knife
rubber spatula
measuring spoons
measuring cup
serving plate
cutting board

Mince beef in blender. Add all ingredients except parsley. Blend well. Form into ball on serving plate. Chop and sprinkle parsley over top and sides. Refrigerate until ready to serve with crackers or cucumber slices.

Time: 3-5 minutes

MILD PATE BALL

A cinch to make, and its delicate, subtle flavor appeals to just about everyone. Can be made a day in advance.

INGREDIENTS
1 3-oz. package of cream cheese
  at room temperature
1 4¾-oz. can Sell's liver paté
4 tsp. dry sherry or dry vermouth
1 tsp. lemon juice
1/2 c. fresh parsley, minced

UTENSILS
small bowl
can opener
measuring spoons
measuring cup
spreader
paring knife
serving plate
cutting board

Thoroughly blend first 4 ingredients in small bowl. Form paté into ball on serving plate. Mince parsley and sprinkle over ball until thoroughly covered. Refrigerate until ready to serve with mild crackers, such as Bremner Wafers.

Time: 3-5 minutes

CURRIED EGG SALAD

It's the combination of curry and fresh herbs that makes this the most attractive and delicious egg salad you've ever tasted. Increase the quantity and make it a day ahead for a party. Leftover makes a phenominal sandwich.

INGREDIENTS
2 eggs
3 tbsp. Hellmann's mayonnaise
1/2 tsp. salt
1/8 tsp. pepper
1/4 tsp. curry powder, dissolved in
  1/2 tbsp. water
2 tbsp. minced celery stalk and
  celery leaves
1/2 tsp. each of fresh, chopped
  tarragon, oregano, chives,
  basil, parsley, etc.

UTENSILS
small saucepan
egg slicer
2-c. measuring jar with
  lid
measuring spoons
tablespoon
fork
paring knife
cutting board

Cover eggs in saucepan with hot water. Boil 12 minutes. Meanwhile measure mayonnaise into jar. Mince celery and herbs. Add salt, pepper, celery, herbs, and dissolved curry to jar. Stir mixture well with fork. When eggs are done, drain and peel under cold water. Slice both ways with egg slicer directly into jar. Stir with fork until blended. Cover and refrigerate until ready to serve on baby pumpernickle slices, mild crackers, or cucumber rounds.

Time: 20 minutes
Makes: 2/3 cup

CHEESE CUPS

Healthy, refreshing, colorful, and delicious, this cheese mixture can be used to top carrot, turnip, or cucumber slices and used to stuff cherry tomatoes. It is also excellent served with crackers, spread on Swedish Krisprolls, or broiled on English muffins.

INGREDIENTS
4 oz. blue or Roquefort cheese
4 oz. cream cheese
1/8 tsp. freshly ground black pepper
1/2 tsp. salt
1 tsp. lemon juice
1 tsp. brandy
2 tsp. Hellmann's mayonnaise
4 tbsp. fresh chives, chopped
fresh parsley leaves
1/2 c. walnuts, chopped
2 9" zucchini

UTENSILS
medium mixing bowl
fork
paring knife
cutting board
measuring spoons
melon baller
nut chopper or blender
 or food processor
teaspoon

Add blue cheese to bowl and crumble with fork. Add cream cheese, pepper, salt, lemon juice, brandy, and mayonnaise. Mix vigorously with fork. Chop walnuts. Stir nuts and chives into cheese mixture.

Cut zucchini into slices 1/2" thick. Use melon baller to scoop out a neat hollow in the center of each slice. Take heaping teaspoon and mound cheese in center. Dot with fresh parsley leaf. Refrigerate or serve.

Time: 20 minutes
Makes: 36 cheese cups

ONION SQUARES

So fancy and flavorful, it's hard to believe this is so simply made from ingredients usually on hand.

INGREDIENTS
4 slices Melba-thin white bread,
   crusts removed
4 1" white pearl (or sweet red)
   onions, cut in 1/8" slices
Hellmann's mayonnaise
salt
pepper
grated Parmesan cheese

UTENSILS
paring knife
cookie sheet
cutting board
metal spatula

Preheat oven to 450°.

Spread crustless bread with thin layer of mayonnaise. Cut each slice into ninths and place on cookie sheet. Top each piece with 1 slice of onion, salt, pepper, a dot of mayonnaise, and a bit of Parmesan cheese. Broil squares about 3 minutes or until golden and bubbly.

Time: preparation: 7 minutes
broiling: 3 minutes
Makes: 36 squares

CHEESE AND CHUTNEY COOKIES

Most people don't think of combining cheese and chutney. In cookie form they are delicious and very easy to eat.

INGREDIENTS
2/3 c. Bisquick biscuit mix
1 5-oz. jar cheese-and-bacon or
Old English Cheddar spread
4 tbsp. melted butter
2 tbsp. fresh parsley, minced
chutney

UTENSILS
small bowl
measuring spoons
fork
cookie sheet
paring knife
cutting board
butter melter or small
saucepan

Preheat oven to 400°.
Blend all ingredients but chutney in bowl with fork. On ungreased cookie sheet drop teaspoon-sized portions of mixture. Top each "cookie" with a chunk of chutney. Bake 10-12 minutes. Serve hot.

Time: preparation: 8-10 minutes
baking: 10-12 minutes
Makes: 20 cookies

OLIVE PUFFS

An elegant hors d'oeuvre that everyone devours swiftly. Takes organization and concentration to prepare in the allotted time, but is well worth the effort. Freezes well.

INGREDIENTS
1 c. Bisquick biscuit mix
1/2 c. grated Parmesan cheese
4 tbsp. cold water
4 tbsp. melted butter
1 tsp. Tabasco sauce
1 7-oz. jar stuffed green olives
paprika

UTENSILS
4 paper towels
large bowl
measuring cup
measuring spoons
cookie sheet
butter melter or small
saucepan
fork

Preheat oven to 400°.

Drain olives and pat dry on paper towels. Mix first 5 ingredients in bowl with fork. Mold enough dough around each olive to cover it. Place balls on cookie sheet and sprinkle paprika on top. Bake 10-15 minutes or until balls are lightly browned. Add 5 minutes to cooking time if balls have been frozen.

Time: preparation: 15-20 minutes
      baking: 10-15 minutes
Makes: 40-50 puffs

DEVILED MEATBALLS

These delightfully different meatballs are also great when served over noodles as a main dish for two. Freezes well.

INGREDIENTS	UTENSILS
1/2 4½-oz. can deviled ham	large mixing bowl
1 egg	measuring cup
1/2 c. bread crumbs	measuring spoons
1/4 tsp. salt	fork
1/8 tsp. pepper	large skillet
2 heaping tsp. prepared mustard	platter or plate
2 tbsp. fresh parsley, minced	paring knife
1/2 tsp. dried dill weed	cutting board
1/2 lb. ground beef	mixing spoon
1 tbsp. butter	wire whisk
2 tbsp. vegetable oil	
1/2 10-oz. can Campbell's Cream of Mushroom Soup	
1/4 c. water	
1 heaping tsp. prepared mustard	

Mince parsley. Mix first 8 ingredients with fork in large bowl. Add beef and mix well again. Form into 1″ balls. Meanwhile start heating butter and oil in skillet over medium-high heat. When butter is bubbly, add meatballs as you can and brown them, being careful not to let them touch as they cook. Remove browned balls to platter. Drain fat from pan and add soup, water, and mustard. Stir well with whisk. Return meatballs to skillet and gently coat them with sauce.

Time: preparation: 10 minutes
      cooking: 10 minutes
Makes: 3½ dozen

HOT SAUSAGE PUFFS

Our friends agree that this is the best variation they've ever tasted.
Freezes well.

INGREDIENTS
1/2 lb. Park's Hot & Sagey sausage
1½ c. Bisquick biscuit mix
2 c. Cheddar cheese, grated
1/4 c. onion, minced
1/4 c. fresh parsley, minced

UTENSILS
large bowl
1-qt. measuring pitcher
cheese grater
paring knife
cutting board
cookie sheet
2 forks

Preheat oven to 400°.
    Grate cheese; mince onion and parsley. Put all ingredients in bowl, and mix thoroughly with your hands. Form into 1/2″ balls. Place balls on cookie sheet. Cook 10 minutes or until golden and puffy. Add 5 minutes to cooking time—turning once after 10 minutes—if balls have been frozen.

Time: preparation: 20 minutes
          baking: 10 minutes
Makes: 80 puffs

ONION-CHEESE STUFFED MUSHROOMS

This unusual combination of flavors makes a delicious and showy first course or hors d'œuvre which can be made in advance.

INGREDIENTS
6 medium or 4 large fresh
    mushrooms
1½ tbsp. butter
1 tbsp. bread crumbs
1 tbsp. lemon juice
1/8 tsp. cayenne pepper
1/8 tsp. salt
1 small onion, finely chopped
2 tbsp. fresh parsley, minced
3 tbsp. whipping or sour cream
1 1-oz. slice Gruyère or
    Swiss cheese, cut into 4 or 6
    squares, depending upon the
    number of mushrooms used

UTENSILS
2 paper towels
paring knife
cutting board
measuring spoons
small skillet
mixing spoon
small baking dish

Preheat oven to 450°. Grease baking dish with 1/2 tbsp. butter.
    Wipe mushrooms clean with damp paper towels. Put caps hollow up in baking dish. Remove stems and thoroughly chop them. Mince parsley and

onion. Melt remaining butter in skillet over medium heat. Sauté mushroom stems and onion 1-2 minutes. Add cream, parsley, lemon juice, bread crumbs, salt, and cayenne pepper to skillet. Stir to combine. Remove from heat. Spoon mixture into mushroom caps. Top each cap with a cheese square.* Bake 8-10 minutes, or until cheese melts.

Time: 16-18 minutes
Serves: 2

*Can be prepared in advance to this point.

TINY CHEESE SQUARES

Very pretty, different, and delicious. Increase the quantity or serve with a salad for a light lunch.

INGREDIENTS	UTENSILS
3 slices Melba-thin white bread	large skillet
3 tbsp. butter	paring knife
4 tbsp. vegetable oil	measuring spoons
1 egg	measuring cup
1 tsp. salt	metal spatula
1/4 tsp. pepper	fork
1/2 c. bread crumbs	2 small bowls
1 tbsp. fresh parsley, minced	cutting board
2 oz. Swiss cheese (or Gruyère or mozzarella)	
1/2 lemon, sliced in half lengthwise	

Slice cheese thin. Remove crusts from bread. Butter inside of each slice. Make 1½ cheese sandwiches. Cut large sandwich in fourths. Cut half sandwich in half. This makes 6 squares. Put leftover butter and 2 tbsp. olive oil in skillet and turn heat to medium high. Meanwhile in one bowl mix egg and 2 tbsp. olive oil. In other bowl mix bread crumbs, salt, pepper, and parsley. Dip each sandwich square into egg mixture and then into breadcrumb mixture. Sauté all 6 squares in skillet, turning once, until golden brown. Serve 3 squares to each person. Garnish each plate with a lemon quarter.

Time: preparation: 6-8 minutes
        cooking: 6 minutes
Serves: 2

SOUPS

COLD FRUIT SOUP

The perfect first course for a summer luncheon or dinner party.

INGREDIENTS
1 10-oz. package Bird's Eye
  "quick thaw" mixed fruits
1/4 c. rum
1 tbsp. lemon juice
1/8 tsp. cinnamon

UTENSILS
blender or food
  processor
measuring cup
measuring spoons

Put plastic bag of fruit under warm running water for 1 minute, or just long enough to break up fruit pieces. Put contents of bag into blender. Add remaining ingredients and blend 30-60 seconds or until smooth. Refrigerate until ready to serve in chilled bowls. Garnish with mint leaves or a slice of fresh strawberry.

Time: 3 minutes
Serves: 2-4

GAZPACHO

A superb soup for a hot summer's day, and it can be ready to serve in 5 minutes if your juice has been pre-chilled.

INGREDIENTS
1 6-oz. can V-8 juice
1 green onion, sliced
4 1" squares green pepper
2 1/4" slices cucumber or
  1 tsp. fresh chives, chopped
1/8 tsp. garlic powder
1/2 tsp. salt
1/4 tsp. pepper
1/2 tsp. wine vinegar
1 tsp. olive oil

UTENSILS
can opener
cutting board
paring knife
measuring spoons
blender or food
  processor

Cut onion, green pepper, and cucumber as directed. Put all ingredients into blender and blend on high speed for 5-10 seconds (until chopped fine but not perfectly smooth). You may serve immediately if you have used chilled juice. If you have not, put soup either into freezer for 20-25 minutes or into refrigerator for one hour. Serve soup in chilled mugs or bowls. Garnish with a cucumber slice or chopped chives.

Time: preparation: 5 minutes
       chilling: 20-25 minutes in freezer
Serves: 2

FRESH TOMATO SOUP

A treat for tomato-lovers and a life-saver for tomato-growers.

INGREDIENTS
1/2 c. water
1 beef boullion cube
2 tbsp. sugar
1/2 tsp. salt
2 c. fresh tomatoes, cubed (about
    2 large tomatoes)
1 tsp. fresh basil, minced, or
    1/4 tsp. dried basil
1 tbsp. fresh parsley, minced
1 tsp. fresh chives, chopped
1 tbsp. cornstarch
1 tbsp. water

UTENSILS
2 qt. saucepan with lid
paring knife
cutting board
measuring spoons
measuring cup
mixing spoon
blender or food
    processor

Put first 4 ingredients into saucepan over high heat while you cube the tomatoes and mince the herbs. Add tomatoes, basil, and parsley to pot and bring to a boil while stirring constantly. Cover and cook 5 minutes over medium-high heat. Turn heat to low and cook 5 minutes more. Meanwhile measure cornstarch and water into measuring cup and blend thoroughly with spoon. Pour hot tomato mixture into blender, cover securely, and blend on high speed for 15 seconds. Return tomato liquid to saucepan (through a strainer if you object to a few tomato seeds). Stir cornstarch mixture into the soup. Return saucepan to high heat. Stir constantly until liquid comes to a boil. Pour into serving bowls, garnish with the chopped chives, and serve.

Time: 15-18 minutes
Serves: 2-4

BEEF BOULLION SUPREME

Even without homemade stock you can have a beautiful boullion.

INGREDIENTS
1½ c. water
3 beef boullion cubes
1 carrot
2 tbsp. onion, minced
2 sprigs fresh parsley
1/4 tsp. celery salt
1 bay leaf
1/4 c. red Burgundy wine
2 tsp. dry sherry
2 slices lemon

UTENSILS
small saucepan with lid
measuring cup
measuring spoons
paring knife
vegetable peeler
mixing spoon
small strainer
cutting board

Put water and boullion cubes into saucepan on high heat. Peel and slice carrot very thin and mince the onion. Break up boullion cubes with spoon. Add carrot slices, onion, parsley, celery salt, bay leaf, and Burgundy to saucepan. Cover and cook 10 minutes over low heat. Hold strainer over each serving bowl and pour half of the liquid into each. Discard cooked vegetables. Add 1 tsp. dry sherry to each bowl and mix. Garnish each bowl with a lemon slice.

Time: 15 minutes
Serves: 2

LIMA BEAN SOUP

This recipe transforms perfectly dreadful canned lima beans into a sensational soup, which is hearty enough to make a meal when served with bread and a salad.

INGREDIENTS	UTENSILS
1 16-oz. can green lima beans	medium saucepan with
3 strips bacon, cut into 1″ slices	lid
1 small onion, chopped	paring knife
1 c. milk	measuring spoons
1 tsp. salt	cutting board
1/8 tsp. pepper	slotted spoon
	can opener
	blender or food
	processor and
	measuring cup
	paper towel

Sauté bacon in saucepan until brown and crisp. Remove bacon with slotted spoon and drain on paper towel. Add onion to bacon fat in saucepan and sauté until golden. Add undrained lima beans. Cover and cook on high heat 4-5 minutes. Measure milk into blender and add cooked bean mixture. Cover securely and blend on high speed for 10-15 seconds. Return to saucepan and bring to a boil over medium-high heat before serving. Top with crumbled bacon at serving time.

Time: 12-15 minutes
Serves: 2-4

CREAM OF FRESH ASPARAGUS SOUP

This soup is one of the delights of "fresh asparagus time". It turns the broth and tough ends, which are usually thrown away, into one of the most delicious soups you may ever taste.

INGREDIENTS
2 tbsp. butter
2 tbsp. flour
1/4 tsp. celery salt
1/4 tsp. onion powder
1/8 tsp. white pepper
1 chicken boullion cube
1½ c. asparagus broth with cut
    ends (see Index for Fresh
    Asparagus)
2 tbsp. whipping cream

UTENSILS
medium saucepan with
    lid
measuring spoons
measuring cup
mixing spoon

Put first 6 ingredients into saucepan on medium heat. Stir constantly until well blended. Add asparagus broth and pieces. Turn heat to high and stir constantly until thickened. Add cream and stir. Remove from heat. Cover.

Time: 5 minutes
Makes: approximately 2 cups

CREAM OF SPINACH SOUP

Probably the easiest and most delicious spinach soup you've ever tried. Equally good hot or cold.

INGREDIENTS
1 10-oz. package frozen spinach
    or broccoli or cauliflower
2 chicken boullion cubes
1 small onion, chopped
1 c. water
1/4 tsp. salt
1/8 tsp. pepper
1/8 tsp. ground nutmeg
1/2 c. milk
1/2 c. whipping cream

UTENSILS
2-qt. saucepan with lid
paring knife
measuring cup
measuring spoons
mixing spoon
blender or food
    processor

Put first 4 ingredients into saucepan and bring to a boil. Cover and cook 10 minutes on medium heat, stirring occasionally to break up spinach. Pour contents of saucepan into blender, cover securely, and blend 10 seconds on high speed. Mixture should be smooth. Return mixture to saucepan. Add remaining ingredients and bring to a boil. Serve hot or refrigerate to serve cold later. Garnish with a lemon slice or a teaspoon of sour cream.

Time: 10-12 minutes
Serves: 2-4

20

CHICKEN A LA REINE

You will hardly believe this could be canned soup!

INGREDIENTS
1 10-oz. can Campbell's Cream of
   Chicken (or Mushroom)
   Soup
1/2 soup can hot water
1 chicken boullion cube
1/8 tsp. cayenne pepper
1/8 tsp. onion powder
1/2 tsp. lemon juice
1/2 tsp. Worcestershire sauce
2 tsp. dry sherry or dry white
   wine

UTENSILS
can opener
medium saucepan
wire whisk
measuring spoon

Put all ingredients into saucepan over medium heat and beat with wire whisk until smooth. Bring to a boil and cook 1 minute.

Time: 5 minutes
Serves: 2

ONION SOUP

Savory French onion soup . . . a delicious beginning to any meal or a great main dish for lunch.

INGREDIENTS
2 tbsp. butter
2 medium-large onions
   (approximately 1½ c.), halved
   and sliced thin
1½ c. water
1/2 c. dry vermouth or white wine
1 tsp. onion powder
4 beef boullion cubes
1/4 tsp. dried thyme

UTENSILS
large, sharp knife
cutting board
1½ qt. saucepan with
   lid
measuring spoons
2-c. measuring pitcher
mixing spoon

Melt butter in saucepan over medium-high heat while you halve and slice the onions and add them to saucepan. Sauté onions 5 minutes. Turn heat to high and add remaining ingredients. Bring to a boil, stir, and cover. Reduce heat to medium and simmer 15 minutes. At serving time top with croutons, Parmesan Bread Cubes (see Index), grated Parmesan, or shredded Gruyère cheese.

Time: sautéing: 10 minutes
       cooking: 15 minutes
Serves: 2-4

THE VICHYSSOISES

One can make a simple soup of this kind from almost any vegetable and enjoy the soup either hot or cold. The variations that follow are based upon the most delicious one of them all – Watercress Vichyssoise – and any one of them would make the perfect do-it-ahead soup course for a dinner party.

WATERCRESS VICHYSSOISE

INGREDIENTS
2 c. water
3 chicken boullion cubes
1 tsp. salt
1/2 tsp. white pepper
2 medium Idaho potatoes, peeled
   and diced very small
1/2 bunch watercress, washed,
   with largest stems removed
   and several leaves set aside
   for garnish
1 heaping tbsp. onion, minced
3/4 c. whipping cream
3/4 c. milk

UTENSILS
2-qt. saucepan with lid
measuring cup
measuring spoons
paring knife
vegetable peeler
cutting board
metal spatula
mixing spoon
blender or food
   processor
2-c. jar with lid

Put water, boullion cubes, salt, and pepper in saucepan over high heat. Peel and dice potatoes and add to pot as each potato is finished, along with onion and then watercress. (Metal spatula is a great tool for scooping up the diced bits quickly.) Cover and boil for 10 minutes. Do not drain. Add milk, cream, and potato mixture to blender. Blend on high speed until smooth. Return half to pot and bring to boil to serve hot. Garnish with a couple of watercress leaves or parsley bits. Put remaining half in jar and refrigerate to serve cold the next night.

Time: 25-30 minutes
Serves: 4

APPLE VICHYSSIOSE

Use 1 medium Idaho potato instead of 2. In place of watercress, use 2 small apples, cored, peeled (but reserve peels), and diced. Add apple chunks and peels with the potato and cook as directed. Discard apple peels before putting everything into the blender.

CARROT VICHYSSOISE

Use 1 medium Idaho potato instead of 2. In place of watercress, use 4 large carrots, washed with a scrub brush, unpeeled, and sliced. Add slices with the potato and cook as directed.

CAULIFLOWER VICHYSSOISE

In place of the watercress, use 1 10-oz. package of frozen cauliflower. Cook as directed. Garnish with ground nutmeg.

CUCUMBER VICHYSSOISE

In place of the watercress, use 3 8″ cucumbers, halved, with seeds removed, diced small. Use 1 Idaho potato instead of 2. Use 2 tablespoons minced onion instead of 1. Cook as directed.

PARSLEY VICHYSSOISE

In place of the watercress, use 1 fully packed cup of parsley sprigs. Cook as directed.

SPINACH VICHYSSOISE

In place of the watercress, use 2½ oz. fresh spinach (about 2 cups). Spinach should be washed, with largest stems removed. Cook as directed.

ZUCCHINI VICHYSSOISE

In place of the watercress, use 1 10″ zucchini, halved, with seeds removed, diced small. Add 1 heaping tablespoon fresh, chopped basil. Cook as directed.

CHEESE SOUP

Served with a salad and dessert, this is a nutricious, quick, and tasty meal.

INGREDIENTS
5 tbsp. butter
2 slices bread, cut into 1/4"
    cubes
1/4 c. onions, finely minced
1 small stalk celery, finely minced
2 tbsp. flour
3/4 tsp. salt
3 dashes cayenne pepper
1/8 tsp. garlic powder
1 c. chicken stock (or 1 chicken
    boullion cube dissolved in
    1 c. hot water)
1 c. milk
5 oz. Swiss cheese, shredded
    (about 1¼ c.)
1 oz. Cheddar cheese, shredded
    (about 1/4 c.)
1 tbsp. fresh parsley, minced
2 Holland rusks or 2 slices toast

UTENSILS
2-qt. saucepan
paring knife
cutting board
measuring spoons
measuring cup
small bowl
cheese grater
2 soup bowls

Cube bread. Melt 2 tbsp. butter in saucepan over low heat and sauté bread cubes until lightly browned. Meanwhile mince onions and celery. Remove croutons to bowl. Melt remaining butter in saucepan and sauté onions and celery until tender, but not brown. Mince parsley and grate cheese. Add flour, salt, pepper, and garlic powder to pan and stir. Turn heat to high. Add chicken stock and stir swiftly and constantly until sauce thickens. Add milk and stir until sauce begins to boil. Reduce heat to medium high. Add cheese and parsley. Stir constantly until cheese melts and soup is smooth. Place rusks in soup bowls and pour soup over them. Top with croutons and serve.

Time: 20 minutes
Serves: 2-4

ENTREES

ALMOND FETTUCINI

Almonds and parsley make this a unique and scrumptuous version of an economical and filling favorite.

INGREDIENTS
2 qts. hot water
4 c. uncooked wide egg noodles
1 tsp. salt
1 egg yolk
1/2 c. sour cream
2 tbsp. fresh parsley, minced
1/4 tsp. freshly ground
    black pepper
1/4 c. slivered almonds
4 tbsp. melted butter
1/2 c. grated Parmesan cheese

UTENSILS
4-qt. saucepan
measuring spoons
mixing spoon
bowl
paring knife
colander or large
    strainer
2-c. measuring cup
butter melter or small
    saucepan

Bring 2 qts. hot water to a boil in saucepan. Meanwhile mince parsley. Add salt and noodles to water and boil 7 minutes. In pitcher measure sour cream and then cheese; stir in egg yolk, parsley, pepper, and almonds. Melt butter. Drain noodles. Return noodles to saucepan. Stir in butter and sour-cream mixture. Cook over medium heat for 2 minutes, stirring constantly. Serve immediately on heated plates.

Time: 12-15 minutes
Serves: 2

PASTA SALAD

Delectable and different, this is a treat for both hostess and guest since it can be made in advance and should be served at room temperature. Add a cup of cooked cubed chicken, seafood, or kidney beans to stretch or change the flavor and substance.

INGREDIENTS
1/2 lb. rotelle or linguine
1 tsp. salt
1 6-oz. jar marinated artichoke
    hearts, drained
6 pitted ripe olives, sliced
6 pimento-stuffed green olives,
    sliced
1 small green pepper, sliced in
    thin strips
1/2 6-oz. package frozen Chinese
    pea pods
1/2 20-oz. can cooked garbanzo
    beans

UTENSILS
4-qt. pot
paring knife
cutting board
measuring spoons
can opener
colander or large
    strainer
large bowl
2 mixing spoons

DRESSING:
1/3 c. Dijon Dressing (see Index)
1/4 tsp. curry powder
1/8 tsp. garlic powder

Cook pasta according to package directions, until done al dente. Drain pasta in colander and run under cold water to bring it to room temperature.

Meanwhile slice olives, pepper, and artichoke hearts. Add these and snow peas and garbanzo beans to large bowl. Add dressing and mix. Toss in pasta and stir lightly to distribute dressing evenly. Serve.

Time: 15-20 minutes
Serves: 2-4

SPAGHETTI A LA CARBONARA

A taste this different and delicious should not be so easy, but it is. You will want to serve our version again and again.

INGREDIENTS	UTENSILS
1/3 lb. spaghetti (#9 or linguine)	4-qt. pot
2 qt. hot water	large skillet
1 tsp. salt	2 forks
6 strips thick bacon	serving spoon
1/4 c. butter	3 paper towels
2/3 c. grated Romano or	measuring spoons
Parmesan cheese	measuring cup
1/4 c. dry vermouth or white wine	colander or large
1/4 tsp. freshly ground	strainer
black pepper	
3 tbsp. green onions or chives,	
chopped	
2 tbsp. parsley, chopped	

Put hot water in pot over high heat and bring to boil. Add salt and spaghetti and cook 8 minutes.

Meanwhile fry bacon over medium heat until nicely crisp and brown. Remove from pan and drain on paper towels. Drain fat from pan. Add butter and melt over low heat. Crumble bacon on paper towel.

When spaghetti is cooked, drain and return to pot. Add half the melted butter to spaghetti and stir with fork. Stir in cheese.

To remaining butter in skillet add bacon, vermouth, and pepper. Bring to boil over high heat. Add onions and parsley, stir, and bring to boil. Pour sauce into spaghetti, stir, and serve immediately on warmed plates.

Time: 25 minutes
Serves: 2

TORTELLINI TAKE-OFF

This has the taste and yummy goodness of tortellini without the major time and effort true tortellini requires.

INGREDIENTS
4 oz. macaroni shells
  (2 c. uncooked)
2 qt. hot water
1 tsp. salt
1/4 c. butter
2 boneless chicken breasts
1 tbsp. Wondra granulated flour
1/4 tsp. salt
1/8 tsp. white pepper
2 oz. cream cheese
3/4 c. whipping cream
1 tbsp. brandy
2 tbsp. lemon juice
2 tbsp. fresh parsley, minced
3 tbsp. fresh chives, chopped
1/2 c. grated Parmesan cheese

UTENSILS
3-qt. saucepan
measuring cup
measuring spoons
paring knife
cutting board
serving spoon
fork
large skillet
3 paper towels
small bowl
colander or large
  strainer

Put hot water on to boil over high heat. As soon as water is boiling rapidly, add 1 tsp. salt and macaroni. Stir, reduce heat to medium, and cook 15-18 minutes or until just tender.

Meanwhile, melt 4 tbsp. butter and pour into small bowl; set aside. Put remaining 4 tbsp. butter to melt in skillet over low heat while you wash and pat dry the chicken breasts. Sprinkle 1/2 tsp. granulated flour over top side of each breast and place floured side down in buttery skillet over medium heat. Sprinkle remaining flour over top side of breasts. Sauté each side 1 minute, remove skillet from heat, and cut chicken into 1/2" squares. Add salt, pepper, and cream cheese to skillet. Mash cream cheese with fork. Add cream, lemon juice, and brandy. Blend over low heat, stirring until smooth.

Wash, dry, and prepare parsley and chives.

When macaroni is cooked, drain and return to pot. Stir melted butter in with fork. Stir in Parmesan cheese. Stir herbs into sauce, mix hot cream-and-chicken sauce with pasta over low heat, and serve immediately on warmed plates.

Time: 30 minutes
Serves: 2

CURRIED CRAB PIE

This is a very filling dish. Accompanied by a salad, it could easily serve 6 for lunch. Alone, as an appetizer, it could serve 8-10. Cover unused portion tightly with foil and refrigerate. To reheat, pop pie into 425° oven and heat 10 minutes or until hot; do not let crust burn.

INGREDIENTS
1 frozen pie crust
1 6-oz. package of frozen crab
    meat, thawed, with excess
    liquid squeezed out of bag
1 8-oz. package cream cheese at
    room temperature
6 tbsp. Hellmann's mayonnaise
1½ tsp. curry powder
1/2 tsp. white pepper
1½ tsp. salt
5 tsp. lemon juice
1/3 c. chopped walnuts

UTENSILS
1½-qt. saucepan
measuring spoons
fork
rubber spatula
nut chopper or food
    processor
mixing spoon

Preheat oven to 425°. Drain crab meat. Chop walnuts. Prick pie crust with fork and bake 5 minutes.

Meanwhile mix crab meat, cream cheese, mayonnaise, curry, pepper, salt, lemon juice, and half the chopped walnuts in the saucepan. Heat over medium-high heat, stirring constantly until mixture is hot and pie crust is cooked. Remove pie crust from oven and turn oven temperature down to 375°. Smooth crab mixture into crust. Sprinkle remaining chopped walnuts on top. Bake 15 minutes. Slice and serve.

Time: preparation: 5 minutes
        baking: 15 minutes
Serves: 6

ASPARAGUS CHEESE PUFF

An elegant luncheon or supper dish. Omit the ham, and it makes a very pretty and filling first course.

INGREDIENTS
1 tsp. butter
2 slices boiled ham
6 asparagus spears, canned or
    leftover cooked fresh
    (see Index)
2 1-oz. slices Gruyère cheese
4 eggs

UTENSILS
2 au gratin dishes or
    individual
    casseroles
measuring cup
measuring spoons
cheese grater
fork

1/2 c. whipping cream
1/4 tsp. salt
1/8 tsp. cayenne pepper
1/2 c. grated Cheddar cheese

Preheat oven to 375°.
   Use the 1 tsp. butter to coat the insides of the 2 au gratin dishes. Place 1 slice of the ham and Gruyère cheese in each dish. Top each with 3 asparagus spears. Measure cream into measuring cup; add egg and beat with fork. Divide the mixture evenly over asparagus in each dish. Grate Cheddar cheese and sprinkle on top. Bake 20 minutes or until puffed and golden brown. Serve at once; the puff falls quickly.

Time: preparation: 5 minutes
        baking: 20 minutes
Serves: 2

CHEESE RAREBIT

This often-neglected old favorite is quick, economical, hearty, and delicious: the perfect lunch for a cold and windy day.

INGREDIENTS
2 tbsp. butter
2 tbsp. flour
1/4 tsp. salt
1/8 tsp. cayenne pepper
1 tsp. dry mustard
3/4 c. milk
1/4 c. dry white wine
1/2 tsp. Worcestershire sauce
1/2 lb. sharp Cheddar
    cheese, cut into
    cubes
1 egg yolk*
4 slices bread

UTENSILS
paring knife
1½-qt. saucepan
cutting board
measuring spoons
mixing spoon
fork
measuring cup
toaster

Toast bread. Melt butter in saucepan over high heat. Add flour, salt, pepper, and mustard and stir constantly until blended. Add milk; stir swiftly until sauce comes to a boil. Reduce heat to medium. Stir in wine and Worcestershire sauce. Add cheese cubes and stir until smooth. Remove from heat. Combine one teaspoon hot mixture and egg yolk in measuring cup. Stir egg mixture quickly into hot sauce. Stir 1 minute over low heat. Cut toast into triangles and cover with the cheese sauce. Serve immediately.

Time: 10-15 minutes
Serves: 2

*The egg yolk makes the sauce velvety smooth and thick, but can be eliminated.

31

CHEESE FONDUE

Our combination of cheeses and herbs makes this slightly different from the standard fondue. Served with the suggested vegetables, this makes a very satisfying and complete meal. If mini loaves of French bread are available, use them: their crustiness is delightful.

INGREDIENTS

3/4 lb. imported Jarlsberg cheese,
   shredded
1/4 c. Cheddar cheese, shredded
1 clove garlic, peeled and halved,
   or 1/8 tsp. garlic powder
1¼ c. dry white wine
1/4 tsp. nutmeg, grated
1/8 tsp. white pepper
1/4 tsp. salt
1 tbsp. fresh parsley, minced
1 tsp. fresh oregano, minced
1 tsp. fresh sage, minced
2 tsp. Kirsch
1 tbsp. cold water
2 tsp. cornstarch

1/4 stale loaf French bread, cut
   into 1" cubes (each cube
   should have crust on at least
   one side)
1 c. cherry tomatoes or ham cubes
1 c. cauliflower florets or
   cucumber cubes

UTENSILS

measuring cup
measuring spoons
wooden or stainless
   steel mixing spoon
paring knife
serrated bread knife
cutting board
cheese grater or
   food processor
15" waxed paper
large platter or plate
fondue pot or enameled
   or stainless steel
1½-qt. saucepan

Prepare bread cubes and fresh vegetables and arrange on large serving platter. Shred cheese onto waxed paper.

Rub inside of fondue pot with garlic clove, or add 1/8 tsp. garlic powder later, along with nutmeg. Measure wine into pot; add salt, pepper, and nutmeg; bring to boil over high heat. Meanwhile mince herbs; add herbs, water, Kirsch, and cornstarch to measuring cup; blend well. When wine comes to a boil, add cheese to pot and stir constantly until cheese is thoroughly melted. Then slowly stir in the cornstarch mixture and continue to stir constantly until fondue starts to thicken. Remove fondue pot to sterno stand and serve immediately.

Time: preparation: 5 minutes
        cooking: 12-15 minutes
Serves: 2 very generously

CRUSTLESS QUICHE AU FROMAGE VARIE

Eliminating the crust makes this faster and less fattening than other quiches. The combination of cheeses makes this full-bodied and filling, especially when served with a salad or vegetable.

INGREDIENTS
3/4 c. whipping cream
2 eggs
1/4 tsp. salt
1/8 tsp. white pepper
scant 1/8 tsp. ground nutmeg
3 large sprigs parsley with stems
1 2" square Swiss cheese, cut
    into fourths*
1 1" square Cheddar cheese, cut
    into fourths*
1 tbsp. butter

UTENSILS
measuring spoons
cutting board
paring knife
blender or food
    processor
2 au gratin dishes or
    individual
    casseroles

Preheat oven to 350°.
    Cut cheeses into fourths. Measure cream into blender. Add all other ingredients, except butter, and blend at low speed for 1 minute. Divide mixture evenly between the 2 au gratin dishes. Dot with butter. Bake for 20 minutes or until knife comes out of the center clean. Serve immediately or quiche will fall.

Time: preparation: 3 minutes
            baking: 20 minutes
Serves: 2

*You may use odds and ends of various cheeses to achieve the required amount, but it tastes best if some Swiss and some Cheddar are used.

FRIED MOZZARELLA

Topped by our special Tomato Salsa, this is a fascinating change from the ordinary entrée. It's quick, economical, and absolutely scrumptuous. Serve it with crunchy vegetables or a salad for a main dish. Halve the amounts for an appetizer.

INGREDIENTS
1/2 lb. mozzarella cheese, cut into
    4 slices 1/8" thick
1/4 c. flour
1 egg
1 tbsp. vegetable oil
1½ c. bread crumbs
1 c. vegetable oil
Tomato Salsa (see Index)

UTENSILS
large knife
large, heavy skillet
metal spatula
1 small mixing bowl
2 medium plates
12" aluminum foil
measuring cup

33

Start the Tomato Salsa.

Combine egg and 1 tbsp. oil in mixing bowl, put flour on one plate and bread crumbs on the other. Slice mozzarella cheese. Coat each slice thoroughly first with flour, second with egg mixture, and third with bread crumbs. Lay slices on foil. Chill in freezer for 15 minutes.

Heat oil in skillet until very hot but not smoking. Fry 2-3 minutes on each side, or until color is a nice golden brown. Place two slices on each warm serving plate. Spoon some hot Tomato Salsa on top and serve.

Time: preparation: 5 minutes
        freezing: 15 minutes
        cooking: 4-6 minutes
Serves: 2

SAUSAGE EGGS WITH HORSERADISH SAUCE

Definitely a challenging dish until you master the technique, but worth the effort. The sausage eggs are enticing, most unusual, and absolutely delicious.

INGREDIENTS
2 eggs
6 oz. bulk sausage
1/4 c. flour
1 c. vegetable oil

HORSERADISH SAUCE
1/4 c. sour cream
1 tsp. prepared horseradish
1/8 tsp. salt
1/8 tsp. cayenne pepper
1/4 tsp. onion powder

UTENSILS
2 small saucepans
1-qt. saucepan
1 slotted spoon
1 mixing spoon
measuring spoons
waxed paper
measuring cup
paper towel

Fill small saucepan 3/4 full with water and bring to a boil over high heat. Meanwhile combine all sauce ingredients in small saucepan over lowest heat. Let sit until ready to serve, stirring occasionally. When water boils, add eggs to pan with slotted spoon and let boil for 4 minutes.

Cut 2 8x10" pieces of waxed paper and dust top side lightly with flour. Put half of the sausage on each paper piece and sprinkle lightly with flour. With the heel of your hand push sausage pieces into 4x6" rectangles. Add vegetable oil to 1-qt. saucepan and put on high heat.

When eggs have cooked 4 minutes, run them under cold water and carefully remove the shells. Lightly dust eggs with flour and put each in the center of a sausage rectangle. Gently fold sausage over egg, sealing edges with your fingers. The sausage covering should be larger than the egg and should resemble a turnover. You must be careful with this process or the eggs will break.

Gently lower sausage into hot oil with slotted spoon and cook for 2 minutes on each side or until browned. Drain sausage on paper towel, then serve with warm horseradish sauce.

Time: 20 minutes
Serves: 2

SHIRRED EGGS

This filling dish requires almost no time to prepare, and it's absolutely delicious.

INGREDIENTS
1 tsp. butter
2 slices boiled ham
2 1-oz. slices Gruyère cheese
4 eggs
6 tbsp. whipping cream
salt
pepper
1/4 tsp. dried oregano
1 tbsp. fresh basil or parsley,
    minced

UTENSILS
measuring spoons
paring knife
2 au gratin dishes or
    individual
    casseroles
cutting board

Preheat oven to 350°.

Butter au gratin dishes and into each dish layer 1 slice ham, 1 slice Gruyère cheese, 2 eggs, 3 tbsp. cream. Sprinkle 1/8 tsp. oregano on top of each dish. Salt and pepper. Bake for 10-15 minutes or until whites are set, but yolks are still soft. (Time will be less for wide, shallow dishes.) Meanwhile chop parsley and sprinkle over cooked eggs before serving.

Time: preparation: 2 minutes
         baking: 10-15 minutes
Serves: 2

EGGPLANT BENEDICT

Eggplant deliciously replaces muffins in this version of the classic dish. Even dieters can afford to indulge in this yummy combination.

INGREDIENTS
2 1/2" slices of a medium eggplant
    or large zucchini
3/4 tsp. salt
1/4 tsp. freshly ground black
    pepper
2 tbsp. flour
3/4 c. vegetable oil
2 slices boiled ham
2 slices ripe fresh tomato
2 eggs

UTENSILS
large, heavy skillet
measuring cup
measuring spoons
metal spatula
waxed paper or platter
cookie sheet
blender or food
    processor
medium-sized sharp
    knife
small saucepan
2 paper towels

BLENDER BEARNAISE SAUCE
2 egg yolks at room temperature
1/4 tsp. salt
1/8 tsp. pepper
1/4 tsp. dried tarragon
1 sprig fresh parsley
2 tsp. lemon juice
1½ tsp. red wine vinegar
5 tbsp. hot melted butter

Put 2 egg yolks, 1/4 tsp. salt, 1/8 tsp. pepper, tarragon, and parsley in blender. Put butter in small saucepan on lowest heat. Put oil in skillet over medium-high heat. Place eggplant on waxed paper and sprinkle 1/4 tsp. salt and 2 tbsp. flour over both sides. Fry for approximately 3 minutes or until tender and golden brown on each side. Remove to cookie sheet. Cover with paper towels. Remove skillet from heat. Top eggplant with a slice of ham and a slice of tomato. Sprinkle with 1/4 tsp. salt and 1/8 tsp. freshly ground black pepper. Place in oven on lowest heat. Return skillet to heat and lightly fry 2 eggs (yolks should still be soft). Place eggs on top of eggplant, ham, and tomato; sprinkle with 1/4 tsp. salt and 1/8 tsp. pepper and return cookie sheet to oven.

Put blender on high speed and blend for 5 seconds. Add lemon juice and vinegar and blend for 10 seconds. Add approximately 1/2 tsp. of the hot melted butter and blend for 10 more seconds. Slowly add the remaining butter while blender is constantly on high speed. Turn blender off when all butter is incorporated in the sauce.

Place eggplant stacks on plates and cover with Béarnaise sauce. Serve at once.

Time: 15 minutes
Serves: 2

HAM-AND-CHEESE SANDWICHES
WITH WINE SAUCE

An easy, delicious version of the French Croque Monsieur.

INGREDIENTS	UTENSILS
4 slices bread	large skillet or small
4 slices Muenster cheese	griddle
2 slices boiled ham	metal spatula
1 tbsp. butter	fork
1 tbsp. vegetable oil	measuring spoons
1/2 tsp. salt	measuring cup
1/4 tsp. black pepper	medium mixing bowl
1/3 c. milk	saucepan
1 egg	mixing spoon
	medium ovenproof dish

WINE SAUCE
2 tbsp. butter
2 tbsp. flour
1/4 tsp. salt
1/8 tsp. pepper
1 tbsp. Parmesan cheese
1/2 c. milk
1/3 c. dry white wine

Preheat broiler.

Make 2 sandwiches with 1 slice of ham between 2 slices of cheese on each. Melt butter and oil in skillet over medium heat. Quickly add salt, pepper, milk, and egg to mixing bowl. Beat well with fork. Dip each side of sandwich into this mixture. Sauté sandwiches in skillet 4 minutes on each side while you prepare sauce.

Melt butter in saucepan over high heat. Add flour and stir constantly. Add remaining ingredients, except wine, and stir constantly until smoolth. Add wine and stir until blended. Remove from heat.

Remove sautéed sandwiches to ovenproof dish. Cover with sauce.* Put under broiler until sauce bubbles and begins to brown.

Time: 20-25 minutes
Serves: 2

*Sauce and sandwiches may be prepared to this point a few hours in advance and then refrigerated.

MUSHROOMS ON A MUFFIN

An especially easy and delightful treat for mushroom-lovers.

INGREDIENTS	UTENSILS
1 English muffin, halved	toaster
2 oz. cream cheese	paring knife
2 slices ham	cutting board
15 medium fresh mushrooms,	mixing spoon
sliced	medium skillet
2 tbsp. butter	paper towel

Toast muffin halves. Melt butter in skillet over medium heat. Wipe mushrooms clean with damp paper towel and slice 1/8" thick. Sauté until very lightly browned. Remove from heat. As soon as muffins are toasted, spread each with half the cream cheese. Put 1 slice ham on each and cover with hot mushrooms. Serve immediately.

Time: 5 minutes
Serves: 2

CREAMED BEEF

A lot of bad names have been given to the institutional rendering of this very quick, economical, and delicious dish. Whether for breakfast, lunch, or dinner, whether served over toast or rice, if you try this you will probably serve it often and in a variety of places. For instance, if you can brave bleacher comments, pour the beef into a wide-mouthed thermos and serve it over toast points for a hot, filling meal at a cold football game.

INGREDIENTS	UTENSILS
3 tbsp. butter	1½-qt. saucepan with
1 stalk celery, sliced thin	lid
scant 1/8 tsp. white pepper	paring knife
1 3-oz. package smoked, sliced	cutting board
beef (chopped, pressed, and	mixing spoon
cooked)	measuring spoons
2½ tbsp. flour	measuring cup
1 beef boullion cube	
2/3 c. water	
1 tbsp. sherry or brandy	

Melt 2 tbsp. butter in saucepan over medium-high heat while you slice the celery. Add celery as you can and the pepper. Stir, cover, and cook 4 minutes while you slice the beef thin. Remove cover. Add remaining tbsp. butter, boullion cube, and sliced beef. Cook 1 minute. Sprinkle flour over beef and stir well. Add water and stir constantly until thickened. Add sherry, stir to boil, and serve. Or remove from heat, cover, and let stand until serving.

Time: 12 minutes
Serves: 2

SNEAKY CASSOULET

A real cassoulet takes hours and hours, but our phenominal version is as tasty as it is quick. Leftover lamb, pork, or ham may be substituted and wouldn't need to be cooked so long. You may also boil bones of these meats for additional flavor. Excellent made a day or so in advance; stir gently when reheating.

INGREDIENTS	UTENSILS
2 slices bacon	large, heavy skillet
2 boneless pork chops, cut in	1½-qt. flameproof
1/4"cubes	casserole, or Dutch
1 frankfurter	oven, with lid
1/4 lb. ground lamb	paring knife
1/4 lb. ground pork	slotted spoon
1 small onion, chopped fine	mixing spoon

1 small carrot, sliced very thin
1/4 c. dry white wine
1/2 c. water
2 beef boullion cubes
1/2 tsp. salt
1/4 tsp. freshly ground black
    pepper
1 tbsp. ketchup or tomato paste
1 tbsp. brandy
1 20-oz. can white kidney beans,
    drained (with lid)

measuring spoons
measuring cup
tea ball
cutting board
vegetable peeler

HERB BOUQUET
1 bay leaf
1/4 tsp. thyme leaves
2 cloves garlic, peeled and halved
4 parsley sprigs (or 1/2 tsp. dried)
2 cloves

Cut bacon into 1/2" strips and cook in skillet over medium-high heat while
you cube the pork and slice the frankfurter. Remove cooked bacon to
casserole dish with slotted spoon. Turn heat to high. Sauté pork cubes and
frankfurter slices while you prepare the herb bouquet in the tea ball.
Remove pork and frankfurter to casserole with slotted spoon. Add ground
lamb and pork to skillet and sauté.

Meanwhile add white wine, water, beef boullion cubes, salt, pepper,
ketchup, and herb bouquet to casserole. Bring casserole to boil over high
heat while you cut up carrot and onion. Cover casserole and reduce heat to
low. Remove browned ground meat to casserole with slotted spoon.
Reduce skillet heat to medium-high. Then saute carrot and onion until
tender but not browned. Add vegetables to casserole and stir. Cover and
simmer 5 minutes.

Now add brandy and kidney beans to casserole. Combine *very* gently.
Bring to boil over medium heat and stir once *very* gently. Remove from
heat and serve.

Time: 30 minutes
Serves: 2 very generously

CHILI CON CARNE

This is an easy-going chili that is especially good for a fall or winter brunch and even better made a day or two in advance, so that the flavors can develop fully. Freezes well. For a different and delicious touch, top each serving with a tablespoon of sour cream. Crackers or crusty bread and a crunchy salad are tasty textural additions to the menu.

INGREDIENTS
1 tbsp. butter or oil
1/2 lb. ground beef
1/2 tsp. salt
1/2 envelope Lipton's onion soup
   mix
2 tbsp. chili powder (or more, to
   taste)
1/2 tsp. crushed red pepper corns
1/4 tsp. black pepper
1/4 tsp. cinnamon
1 tbsp. sugar
1 tbsp. cider or red wine vinegar
1 tbsp. tomato paste or ketchup
1 8-oz. can tomatoes with juice,
   cut up
1 20-oz. can kidney beans, drained
   (with lid)

UTENSILS
Dutch oven or large,
   heavy pot or skillet
   with lid
measuring spoons
can opener
mixing spoon

Melt butter in pan over medium-high heat. Add beef and sauté until well browned. Add all other ingredients and stir well. Cover. Reduce heat to low and simmer 15 minutes, stirring occasionally.

Time: 20 minutes
Serves: 2

HONESTLY GOOD HASH

This hamburger-and-potato combination is so good that the only way you'll believe it is to try it.

INGREDIENTS
2 c. water
1 tbsp. oil or butter
1 lb. ground beef
4 medium Idaho potatoes
1 small onion
1/3 c. fresh parsley, chopped
2 tsp. salt

UTENSILS
large, heavy skillet
   with lid
medium saucepan with
   lid
paring knife
chopping board
measuring spoons

1/2 tsp. pepper
4 tsp. Worcestershire sauce
1/2 c. whipping cream
1/2 c. milk
1 tsp. dry mustard
1/4 c. ketchup

2-c. measuring pitcher
mixing spoon

Put water in saucepan over high heat. Peel and dice potatoes fine, putting pieces into the saucepan as you go. Cover and boil for 5 minutes. Melt butter in skillet over high heat. Add hamburger. While meat cooks, dice onion and add to skillet. Stir occasionally. When meat is brown, drain the potatoes and add them to the skillet along with parsley, salt, pepper, and Worcestershire. Measure milk, cream, and ketchup into the measuring cup, and stir in the mustard. Stir this mixture into the skillet. Cover and cook for 5 minutes, stirring occasionally.

Time: 20-25 minutes
Serves: 2 very generously

FONDUE MEATBALLS

Almost as delicious as regular beef fondue, but much less expensive. Don't worry: the meatballs won't fall apart on the fondue forks. If you're not patient enough for fondue, the meatballs can be cooked in 2 tbsp. oil in medium-sized heavy skillet and then served on a platter surrounded by small dishes of sauces.

INGREDIENTS
1 egg
1/2 tsp. celery salt
1 tsp. onion powder
1/4 tsp. black pepper
2 tbsp. fresh parsley, chopped fine
1/4 c. bread crumbs
1/2 lb. ground beef
2 c. vegetable oil

UTENSILS
measuring spoons
measuring cup
large mixing bowl
mixing spoon
fondue pot
fondue forks
paring knife
cutting board

Start heating 2 cups of oil in fondue pot on stove over high heat. Chop parsley. Combine first 6 ingredients with fork in bowl. Add beef and blend well. Form into bite-sized meatballs.* Put one or more of the following sauces in individual dishes: Blender Béarnaise, Dill, Tangy Fruit, Horseradish, or Green Sauce (see Index for sauces). When oil is hot but not yet smoking, transfer pot to fondue stand. Cook and serve.

Time: preparation: 15-20 minutes
Serves: 2

*Can be made a day in advance to this point and frozen.

NUTTY LITTLE MEATBALLS

Almonds provide the crunchy difference in these yummy meatballs. Freezes well. Start rice or noodles immediately if you plan to serve one of them.

INGREDIENTS	UTENSILS
1/4 tsp. pepper	large, heavy skillet
1/2 tsp. salt	large mixing bowl
1/2 tsp. dried oregano	measuring spoons
1 tbsp. fresh parsley, minced	measuring cup
1 tbsp. onion powder	fork
2 tbsp. slivered, crumbled	mixing spoon
almonds	paring knife
1 tbsp. tomato paste or ketchup	cutting board
1 egg	
1/4 c. bread crumbs	
1/2 lb. ground beef	
1 tbsp. butter	
1 tbsp. oil	
1/2 c. sour cream	

Mince parsley. Mix first 9 ingredients in bowl with fork. Add beef and mix well. Form into 1″ balls. Heat butter and oil in skillet over medium-high heat until bubbly. Sauté meatballs, being careful not to let them touch as they cook. When meatballs are browned, remove skillet from heat and stir in sour cream.* Return skillet to medium heat and stir. Do not let mixture boil, or sour cream will curdle.

Time: preparation: 8 minutes
        cooking: 12 minutes
Serves: 2

*Can be made a day in advance to this point.

PEPPER STEAK STROGANOFF

A delicious combination of Chinese Pepper Steak and Russian Stroganoff. It is very good on rice, which should be started beforehand, since this dish is so quickly prepared.

INGREDIENTS	UTENSILS
1/2 lb. boneless sirloin, shoulder,	large, heavy skillet
or other tender steak, sliced	measuring cup
into 1/4″ strips	measuring spoons
3 tbsp. vegetable oil	sharp knife
2 tbsp. butter	cutting board

1/2 green pepper, sliced into 1/2"
   strips
1 onion, sliced thin
1 tomato, cut into 8 wedges
1/2 c. red wine
1 beef boullion cube
1/8 tsp. garlic powder
1 3-oz. can mushrooms with liquid
3 tbsp. sour cream

can opener
mixing spoon
paper towel

Cut beef into strips and pat dry with paper towel. Heat oil and butter in skillet over high heat. Slice vegetables. When oil mixture is very hot, add beef, pepper, and onion and sauté stirring constantly. When beef and onions are browned, add all other ingredients except sour cream and cook uncovered on high heat for 5 minutes. Remove from heat and add sour cream. Stir until well blended and serve.

Time: 15 minutes
Serves: 2

MARINATED STEAKS

Garnish these tasty steaks with fresh watercress or top each steak with an artichoke heart and a tablespoon of Green Sauce (see Index).

INGREDIENTS
1 lb. boneless sirloin, shoulder, or
   other tender steak, cut into
   4 small steaks
1 clove garlic
2 tbsp. lemon juice
2 tbsp. Worcestershire sauce
1 tbsp. soy sauce
1/4 tsp. freshly ground black
   pepper
1 tbsp. vegetable oil
1 tbsp. water

UTENSILS
sharp knife
measuring spoons
plastic container with
   lid or medium
   bowl with cover
2 forks or tongs
heavy skillet
mixing spoon
cutting board

Peel and halve garlic clove lengthwise. Rub both sides of steak with clove. Mix lemon juice, Worcestershire, soy sauce, and pepper in container. Add garlic clove and steaks. Cover and marinate steaks 10 minutes each side. Put oil in skillet over high heat. When oil is hot, but not smoking, and coats bottom of pan, sauté steaks 2 minutes per side. Remove steaks to plates. Add water and marinade to skillet. Stir and bring to boil. Spoon sauce over steaks. Serve.

Time: marinating: 20 minutes
       cooking: 10 minutes
Serves: 2

STEAK AU POIVRE

A simple, quick, and absolutely delicious version of the French classic.

INGREDIENTS
2 club steaks
fresh, coarsely ground black
    pepper
1/4 tsp. salt
2 tbsp. butter
1 tsp. Worcestershire sauce
2 tsp. lemon juice
1/3 c. beef boullion (1/2 beef
    boullion cube dissolved in
    1/3 c. hot water)
1/4 c. fresh parsley, chopped
2 green onions, chopped (or
    1/4 c. yellow onion)
1 tbsp. brandy

UTENSILS
pepper mill
measuring spoons
measuring cup
large, heavy skillet
tongs or large fork
mixing spoon
paring knife
cutting board
waxed paper
match

Place steaks on waxed paper and liberally cover each side of steaks with freshly ground black pepper. Press pepper into the meat with the heel of your hand. Let meat sit 15-20 minutes. Meanwhile chop green onions and parsley. Measure and combine boullion, Worcestershire sauce, lemon juice, and parsley. Sprinkle salt over bottom of skillet over high heat. When salt begins to brown, add steaks. Cook 2 minutes. Reduce heat to medium high. Turn steaks and cook another 2-3 minutes for medium rare. Remove steaks to waxed paper.

Melt butter in skillet over medium-high heat and sauté onions 30 seconds. Add boullion mixture and cook about 1 minute while stirring. (If using yellow onion, cover and cook 2-3 minutes.) Return steaks to skillet. Pour brandy over all. Flame; serve steaks immediately, topped with sauce.

Time: marinating: 15-20 minutes
        cooking: 10 minutes
Serves: 2

SOUTHERN CUBED STEAK

You won't believe that cubed steak can really be so tender and juicy unless you try this. Yummy all by itself, it is great served on a club roll spread with mayonnaise or butter.

INGREDIENTS
1/2 c. flour
1 tsp. salt
1/2 tsp. freshly ground pepper
1/2 c. milk
2 cubed beef steaks
1 c. vegetable oil

UTENSILS
waxed paper
measuring cup
measuring spoons
container with top
large fork or tongs
paper towels
large, heavy skillet
with lid

Put cubed steaks and milk into container and cover. Marinate for 10 minutes. Measure flour and pour onto waxed paper. Add salt and pepper and mix. Heat oil in skillet over high heat. Remove steaks from milk and press flour mixture thoroughly into each side of steak with the heel of your hand. When oil is very hot, but not smoking, add steaks to skillet. Cover and cook 1-1½ minutes on each side depending on the thickness of the steaks. Remove steaks from pan and drain briefly on paper towels, if necessary.

Time: marinating: 10 minutes
        cooking: 5 minutes
Serves: 2

TANGY BARBECUED CHICKEN

Absolutely delicious, and the easiest "barbecued" chicken you'll ever make. As a variation, try this with Elie's Meat Loaf Sauce (see Index).

INGREDIENTS
4 chicken legs or thighs or
  2 chicken breasts
5 tbsp. sweet orange marmalade
3 tbsp. ketchup
1/2 tsp. salt

UTENSILS
broiler pan with rack
measuring spoons
small bowl or cup
mixing spoon
forks or tongs

Preheat broiler. Mix marmalade and ketchup in bowl. Wash chicken and place on broiler rack. Sprinkle with salt. Place broiler pan in oven so that chicken is 5-6" from heat. Broil 4-6 minutes on each side depending on size of chicken pieces. Coat one side of the chicken with sauce and broil 4-5 minutes. Turn chicken; coat remaining side with sauce and broil another 4-5 minutes.

Time: preparation: 2 minutes
        broiling: 16-22 minutes
Serves: 2

CHICKEN CUTLETS BEARNAISE

We've never met anyone who hasn't raved over this simple but elegant dish: it's rich, attractive, and indisputably delicious. Perfect for a dinner party, the breaded cutlets can be frozen in advance.

INGREDIENTS
2 chicken breasts, boneless and
   skinless
1/2 tsp. salt
1/4 c. flour
1 egg
1 tbsp. oil
1/2 c. bread crumbs
3/4 c. vegetable oil

BLENDER BEARNAISE SAUCE
2 egg yolks at room temperature
1/4 tsp. salt
1/8 tsp. pepper
1/4 tsp. dried tarragon
1 sprig fresh parsley
2 tsp. lemon juice
1½ tsp. red wine vinegar
5 tbsp. hot melted butter

UTENSILS
large, heavy skillet
blender or food
   processor
small saucepan or
   butter melter
measuring spoons
measuring cup
fork
waxed paper
ovenproof platter
small bowl
mallet or rolling pin
tongs or 2 forks
paper towel

Turn oven to warm. Put 2 egg yolks, 1/4 tsp. salt, 1/8 tsp. pepper, 1/4 tsp. dried tarragon, and parsley in blender. Put butter in saucepan over lowest heat until melted.

Clean chicken and dry on paper towel. Place the chicken breasts between 2 sheets of waxed paper and pound with mallet until about 1/4" thick. Salt and lightly flour each side of the breasts. Beat 1 egg and 1 tbsp. oil together in small bowl. Dip each breast into the egg mixture and then coat with bread crumbs. Put breaded chicken into the freezer for 10 minutes.

Heat oil in skillet over high heat until very hot but not smoking. Brown chicken cutlets about 1½ minutes per side (chicken should be a rich, golden-brown color). Remove chicken to ovenproof platter and place in oven while preparing Béarnaise sauce.

Turn blender to high and blend 5 seconds; add lemon juice and vinegar and blend for 10 seconds; add approximately 1 tbsp. of the warm butter and blend for 10 more seconds; turn blender to high and slowly add the remaining butter. Turn blender off when all the butter is incorporated into the sauce. Pour sauce over chicken and serve at once.

Time: preparation: 10 minutes
       chilling: 10 minutes
       cooking: 5-10 minutes
Serves: 2

CHICKEN DIJON

This easy chicken recipe, with its heavenly cream sauce, is at its best when served over rice. Start rice before you begin to cook the chicken.

INGREDIENTS
2 chicken breasts, boneless and
   skinless
2 tbsp. butter
4 tbsp. flour
salt
pepper
1/2 c. dry vermouth or white wine
1/3 c. whipping cream
1 tbsp. sour ceam
1 tsp. dry mustard
1 egg yolk

UTENSILS
heavy skillet
measuring spoons
measuring cup
2 forks
paper towel
small plate

Clean chicken breasts and dry on paper towel. Melt butter in skillet over medium-high heat. Salt, pepper, and sprinkle 1 tsp. flour on top side of each breast; put floured side into hot butter. Season and flour top sides in pan. Sauté 2 minutes on each side. Add vermouth and reduce heat to low. Cook 3 minutes on each side. Meanwhile in measuring cup, mix remaining ingredients until smooth. Remove skillet from heat and place breasts on a small plate. Add 2 tbsp. of the hot liquid from the skillet to the mixture in the cup, stirring constantly. Stir the cream mixture into the skillet slowly. Return skillet to medium-high heat and stir until mixture is thick. Add chicken to pan, turning once to coat with sauce. Serve.

Time: 12 minutes
Serves: 2

SUPREME OF CHICKEN
WITH HAM AND CHEESE

Our version of this classic dish couldn't be easier or more delicious.

INGREDIENTS
2 chicken breasts, boneless and
   skinless
2 small slices mozzarella cheese
4 small slices boiled ham
1 egg
4 tbsp. vegetable oil
1/4 tsp. pepper
1/2 tsp. salt
1/4 c. flour
1/2 c. bread crumbs
2 tbsp. dried parsley
1 tbsp. butter

UTENSILS
waxed paper
mallet or rolling pin
4 toothpicks
small, shallow bowl
measuring spoons
heavy skillet
tongs or fork and
   metal spatula
paper towel

Clean chicken breasts and dry on paper towel. Place chicken breasts between 2 sheets of waxed paper and pound with mallet until flat. On one half of each breast layer ham, cheese, ham. Fold over and close with 2 toothpicks. On one end of waxed paper mix flour, salt, and pepper. Roll each breast in flour mixture. Blend egg yolk and 1 tbsp. oil in small bowl. Dip floured breasts into egg mixture. Combine parsley and bread crumbs on waxed paper. Melt butter and oil in skillet over medium-high heat. Roll breasts in bread crumbs* and sauté when butter is bubbly for 4 minutes on each side. Serve.

Time: preparation: 10 minutes
       cooking: 9 minutes
Serves: 2
*Can be made a day in advance to this point or even frozen.

SUPREME OF CHICKEN WITH APPLES

A refreshing and attractive chicken dish that is perfect for a hot summer evening. For a most appealing variation, in place of the apples or grapes use 1/2 of a drained 11-oz. can of mandarin oranges, 1 tbsp. sweet orange marmalade, and 1 tbsp. Triple Sec or Cointreau.

INGREDIENTS	UTENSILS
2 chicken breasts, boneless and skinless	1½-qt. flameproof casserole with lid
1 tbsp. butter	measuring cup
2 tbsp. vegetable oil	measuring spoons
salt	mixing spoon
pepper	cutting board
1 tbsp. Wondra granulated flour	paring knife
1/4 tsp. dried thyme	tongs or 2 forks
1/2 c. chicken stock (1 chicken cube dissolved in 1/2 c. boiling water)	paper towel
1/4 c. dry white wine	
1 small apple, peeled, cored, and sliced thin or 15 white seedless grapes, halved	

Clean chicken breasts and drain on doubled paper towel. Put butter and oil in pot over medium-high heat. Sprinkle salt, pepper, and some of the flour over top of chicken. When butter is bubbly, put chicken flour-side down in pot. Sprinkle more salt, pepper, and flour over top of chicken. Sauté 2 minutes on each side. Add chicken stock, wine, and thyme to pot. Bring to boil, reduce heat to low, stir, cover, and cook 3 minutes on each side.

Meanwhile fix fruit and sprinkle with remaining flour. Just before serving, gently stir in floured fruit. Cook one minute, stirring occasionally. Serve.

Time: 14 minutes
Serves: 2

STUFFED CHICKEN BREASTS

An elegant, easy, and scrumptious way to serve chicken with a very special stuffing.

INGREDIENTS	UTENSILS
1½ slices white bread	small bowl
1/4 tsp. salt	bread knife
1/8 tsp. pepper	cutting board
1/4 tsp. dried thyme	measuring spoons
4 tbsp. soft butter or margarine	measuring cup
2 chicken breasts, boneless and	4 toothpicks
skinless	heavy skillet with lid
1/2 c. chicken stock (1 chicken	mallet or rolling pin
boullion cube in ½ c. water)	paper towel
1 tbsp. lemon juice	waxed paper
1/2 c. whipping cream	
1 tbsp. dry sherry or vermouth	

Clean chicken breasts and dry on paper towel. Stack bread, remove crusts, and slice bread into 1/4" strips, then again crosswise into 1/4" cubes. Put cubes into bowl and mix in salt, pepper, and thyme. Lightly mix in 2 tbsp. of the butter with your fingers. Put chicken between folded waxed paper and pound until flat. Put 1/2 of the stuffing on 1/2 of each chicken breast. Fold other half of breast over and secure edges with 2 toothpicks. Melt remaining 2 tbsp. butter in skillet over medium-high heat. Sauté each stuffed breast about 1 minute on each side. Add chicken stock and lemon juice. Cover and cook 10 minutes, turning chicken once.* Remove breasts to bowl. Turn heat to high and reduce liquid by half. Add cream and stir well to loosen all pan brownings. When sauce is thickened, stir in wine. Add chicken and bring to boil. Turn breasts and remove from heat. Cover until ready to serve.

Time: preparation: 5 minutes
        cooking: 17 minutes
Serves: 2

*Can be made a day in advance to this point or even frozen.

MOCK COQ AU VIN

This jiffy version of chicken in wine sauce is really very good and may be made several days in advance. Serve over rice or noodles which should be started before you begin to cook the chicken.

INGREDIENTS

2 slices bacon
1 tbsp. butter
2 chicken breasts, boneless and
  skinless
1 tbsp. flour
salt
pepper
1 medium onion, in small chunks
1 carrot, sliced thin
1 stalk celery, sliced thin
4 medium mushrooms, wiped
  clean and sliced
3/4 c. Burgundy or other dry red
  wine
3/4 c. stock (3/4 c. hot water +
  1 beef boullion cube +
  1 chicken boullion cube)
1 bay leaf
1/4 tsp. dried thyme
1 clove garlic
1 sprig fresh parsley
1 tbsp. ketchup or tomato paste

UTENSILS

large, heavy skillet
  with lid
measuring spoons
measuring cup
paring knife
cutting board
fork
mixing spoon
slotted spoon
small bowl
tea ball
2 paper towels

Sauté bacon in skillet over medium-high heat. Meanwhile clean chicken and dry on paper towel. Sprinkle one side of breasts with salt, pepper, and flour. Remove bacon to bowl with slotted spoon, add butter to skillet. When butter is bubbly, sauté floured side of chicken while you sprinkle remaining side with salt, pepper, and flour. Sauté about 2 minutes per side. While chicken is cooking, wash and slice vegetables. Remove sautéed chicken to bowl. Add onion, carrot, celery, and mushrooms to skillet. Sauté 2 minutes. Cover and cook 3 minutes, stirring often. Add wine, stock, and chicken breasts to skillet. Stir. Add tea ball which has been filled with bay leaf, thyme, garlic, parsley, and ketchup. Bring to boil. Cover and cook on high heat 7-10 minutes, turning chicken once after 5 minutes. Serve.

Time: 30 minutes
Serves: 2

SOUTHERN FRIED CHICKEN

The secret of our clear-cut version is covered cooking, which eliminates guesswork, lessens mess, and guarantees tender, juicy chicken. The optional gravy works very well and completes this classic Southern treat. If you're going to serve the gravy over rice, mashed potatoes, or noodles, start those starches first.

INGREDIENTS
4 chicken legs or thighs or
   2 chicken breasts
1/2 c. Wondra granulated flour
1/2 tsp. salt
1/4 tsp. freshly ground black
   pepper
2 c. vegetable oil

GRAVY
3 tbsp. Wondra granulated flour
1/4 tsp. salt
1/8 tsp. pepper
1½ c. *hot* water
1 chicken boullion cube, optional

UTENSILS
large, heavy skillet
   with lid
measuring cup
measuring spoons
tongs
waxed paper or platter
3 paper towels
mixing spoon

Put oil in skillet over high heat. Clean chicken; put *wet* chicken pieces on waxed paper. Sprinkle 1/2 of the salt, pepper, and flour on each side of the chicken. Roll chicken in leftover flour that has spilled onto the paper, so that each piece is well coated. When oil is hot, but not smoking, use tongs to carefully lower each piece of chicken into skillet. Cook on high heat for 1 minute. Turn chicken. Reduce heat to medium. Cover and cook 10 minutes. Turn chicken pieces again; recover and cook 8-10 minutes, depending upon the size of the chicken pieces. Remove from skillet and drain on paper towels.

    To make gravy, drain all but 3 tbsp. oil from skillet. Return skillet to high heat and add the first 3 gravy ingredients. Stir constantly until flour is *well* browned. Add hot water and boullion cube, still stirring constantly. Cover and cook on low heat for 1 minute. Stir and serve over rice, mashed potatoes, or noodles, but *not over the chicken.*

Time: preparation: 6-8 minutes
        cooking: 20-22 minutes
Serves: 2

BURGUNDY HAM

This delightful combination of ham, wine, and fruit is ready in less than 10 minutes.

INGREDIENTS
1 tbsp. butter
3/4 lb. precooked ham steak
1 8-oz. can whole cranberry sauce
1/4 c. Burgundy wine

UTENSILS
large, heavy skillet
measuring cup
fork or tongs
mixing spoons
plate
can opener
sharp knife

Melt butter in skillet over high heat. Add ham. Reduce heat to medium high and cook 2 minutes per side. Remove ham to plate and add cranberry sauce and wine to skillet. Stir until well blended. Return ham to skillet and cook for 1 minute on each side. Cut in half, top with sauce, serve.

Time: 7-8 minutes
Serves: 2

HAM IN RUM SAUCE

A very delicious, elegant, and easy way to prepare a standard cut of meat. As a variation, substitute dry white wine for the rum.

INGREDIENTS
3/4 lb. precooked ham steak
1 tbsp. butter
1/2 c. hot water
1 chicken boullion cube
1/4 c. rum
1/2 c. whipping cream
1/4 10-oz. package frozen petite
    peas (or 1/3 c. cooked peas)
1 tbsp. lemon juice
1 tbsp. brandy

UTENSILS
2 paper towels
large, heavy skillet
fork
measuring spoons
measuring cup
mixing spoon
large plate or platter
paring knife

Melt butter in skillet while you rinse off the ham in cold water and pat it dry with the paper towels. Brown ham in skillet over high heat quickly on both sides (about 5 minutes). Meanwhile measure water and rum into measuring cup; add boullion cube and mix with fork. Add chicken stock mixture to skillet and cook ham steak another 5 minutes, turning steak once. Remove steak to plate. Add cream to skillet and blend in all brownings in the pan. Dribble in lemon juice and brandy, stirring all the time. Add peas and stir constantly until sauce starts to thicken. Return ham to pan and cover with sauce. Slice and serve immediately.

Time: 15 minutes
Serves: 2

LAMB CURRY

Add celery along with the onion and apple, if you wish; this dish is very flexible and is best served over rice. Traditional curry condiments (raisins, nuts, coconut, bacon, and chutney, etc.) are welcome, but not essential to this very savory and filling main course. Can be made a day in advance or frozen.

INGREDIENTS	UTENSILS
1 tbsp. bacon fat	large, heavy skillet
3 shoulder lamb chops (or 1¼ c.	paring knife
cooked, sliced lamb)*	measuring cup
1/2 apple, peeled and sliced thin	measuring spoons
2 tbsp. onion, minced fine	mixing spoon
1/4 c. slivered almonds	small bowl
2 tbsp. butter	cutting board
1/4 tsp. powdered ginger	
1 tsp. curry powder	
2 tbsp. flour	
1 c. chicken or beef stock	
(2 boullion cubes in 1 c.	
hot water)	

Start Parsley Rice (see Index).

Melt bacon fat in skillet over medium-high heat while you cut bone, gristle, and fat from chops and cut meat in 1/2" cubes. Sauté cubes. Stir frequently and remove cooked cubes to bowl. Meanwhile prepare onion and apple. When meat is cooked, discard pan fat and stir butter, ginger, and curry powder into skillet. Sauté almonds, onion, and apple until onions are just tender but not brown. Add flour and meat. Stir. Add chicken stock and stir until sauce thickens and comes to a boil. Serve over the cooked rice.

Time: 25 minutes
Serves: 2

*If you're using cooked lamb, you won't have to sauté the meat for as long a time.

BEEF LIVER TRIANGLES

Certainly one of the most economical and nutritious meats you can buy, beef liver becomes a mild, tender, and delicious change of pace when prepared in this manner.

INGREDIENTS	UTENSILS
4 slices bacon	large, heavy skillet
1/2 lb. beef liver	wide, shallow dish
1/2 c. milk	(such as 9" pie
1/3 c. flour	plate)
1/4 tsp. pepper	measuring cup
1/2 tsp. salt	measuring spoons

colander or strainer
tongs or 2 forks
slotted spoon
knife
cutting board
3 paper towels

Cut liver into bite-sized triangles or strips. Put liver into dish and cover with milk. Soak for at least 10 minutes. While liver is soaking in milk, fry the bacon over medium-high heat until crisp. Remove to paper towel. Remove pan from heat. Drain liver in colander. Mix flour, salt, and pepper in dish. Put drained liver back into dish. Coat all sides of liver with flour mixture. Return skillet to high heat. Sauté liver in bacon fat until all pieces are well browned. Remove to paper towel to drain. Top with bacon and serve.

Time: 15 minutes
Serves: 2

PORK AND FRIED RICE

Using standard American ingredients and only one large pan, you can enjoy this economical, delicious, and filling favorite.

INGREDIENTS	UTENSILS
3 tbsp. bacon fat or butter	large, heavy skillet
2 boneless pork chops	with lid
1 large stalk celery, sliced thin	sharp knife
2 green onions, sliced thin	mixing spoon
3/4 c. raw rice	measuring spoons
1¼ c. hot water	measuring cup
1 tsp. salt	cutting board
1/4 tsp. pepper	
1 beef boullion cube	
2 tbsp. soy sauce	
1 egg	

Melt bacon fat in skillet over medium-high heat. Meanwhile cut pork into 1/4″ cubes. When fat is hot, but not smoking, add pork to skillet. Slice celery and sauté along with pork until pork is browned. Slice onions. Turn heat to high. Add rice and onion and sauté until rice is golden. Add water, salt, pepper, and boullion cube. Stir well and bring to a boil. Cover; turn heat to low and cook 12 minutes or until liquid is absorbed.

Meanwhile mix eggs and soy sauce in measuring cup. When rice is cooked, mix in the soy mixture. Stir well, cover, and cook one minute. Remove from heat. Stir. Keep covered until ready to serve.

Time: sautéing: 13 minutes
        cooking: 14 minutes
Serves: 2 generously

54

PORK MEDALLIONS
WITH APPLES AND BEARNAISE SAUCE

A complete change of pace, this very different way to serve pork is both delicious and supremely elegant. It elevates pork from family fare to a memorable dinner-party entrée which is also highly economical.

INGREDIENTS
1/2 lb. boneless pork
4 tbsp. butter
salt
pepper
2 tbsp. flour
1 small onion, chopped fine
1 small carrot, peeled and cut
    into 1/8" slices
2 small tart apples, peeled, cored,
    and cut into quarters
1/2 c. dry white wine
1/2 c. water
1 beef boullion cube
1/2 tsp. fresh sage, minced (or
    1/8 tsp. dried)

UTENSILS
waxed paper
mallet or rolling pin
measuring spoons
measuring cup
paring knife
large, heavy skillet
    with lid
two forks or tongs
mixing spoon
blender or food
    processor
small saucepan or
    butter melter
cutting board

BLENDER BEARNAISE SAUCE
1 egg yolk at room temperature
dash salt
dash pepper
small sprig fresh parsley

1/8 tsp. dried tarragon
1 tsp. lemon juice
3/4 tsp. wine vinegar
2½ tbsp. hot melted butter

Place pork between 2 sheets of waxed paper and pound until pork is approximately 1/4" thick. Cut pork into 4-6 small pieces and lightly salt, pepper, and flour them. Melt 3 tbsp. butter in skillet over medium-high heat. Add pork to skillet and sauté until lightly browned on both sides. Meanwhile prepare onion, carrot, and apple. Remove browned pork to waxed paper. Add 1 tbsp. butter, onion, and carrot to skillet. Sauté until onion is golden. Add apple and sauté 1 minute more. Add wine, water, boullion cube, and sage. Stir well. Return pork to pan, cover, and cook 10 minutes, turning pork and apples once after 5 minutes.

Put egg yolk, dash salt and pepper, parsley, and tarragon into blender. Melt butter in small saucepan.

At serving time, turn blender to high speed for 5 seconds. Add lemon juice and vinegar and blend for 10 seconds. Add approximately 1 tsp. of the melted butter and blend for 10 more seconds. With blender on high speed, slowly add the remaining butter. Turn blender off when all the butter is incorporated into the sauce.

Divide pork, gravy, and apples on 2 plates. Cover with Béarnaise sauce.

Time: 25-28 minutes
Serves: 2

SMOKED PORK CHOPS
WITH CHEESE AND SHERRY

A very pleasant blend of flavors and textures in a recipe that is easy and very quick.

INGREDIENTS	UTENSILS
1 tbsp. butter	large, heavy skillet
2 smoked pork chops (1/2" thick)	pointed paring knife
2 slices mozzarella cheese or	cutting board
2 1/2-oz. chunks of Gruyère	2 toothpicks
1 tbsp. fresh parsley, minced	metal spatula
1 tsp. fresh sage or 1 tbsp. fresh	mixing spoon
basil, minced	measuring spoons
2 tbsp. water	small bowl
1 tbsp. lemon juice	
1 tbsp. sherry	

Melt butter in skillet over medium-high heat. Meanwhile slice cheese and mince herbs. Cut 2" opening to form a deep, wide horizontal pocket in each chop. Insert 1 slice cheese and half the herbs into each pocket. Secure each pocket shut with 1 toothpick. Sauté chops 5 minutes on first side. Measure water, lemon juice, and sherry into small bowl. Before turning chops add liquid to skillet and swirl chops in juices. Turn chops and cook 5 more minutes. Shake pan occasionally. Serve.

Time: 15 minutes
Serves: 2

SPICY STIR-FRY PORK

This zesty Chinese dish is equally delicious made with chicken, beef, or pork. The peanuts and snow peas provide interesting color and texture. This is best served over rice (see Index for Parsley Rice); start the rice first, but use a beef boullion cube and omit the parsley.

INGREDIENTS	UTENSILS
1/2 lb. boneless pork	heavy skillet
2 tbsp. vegetable oil	paring knife
1 tsp. fresh minced ginger (or	cutting board
1/2 tsp. dried)	measuring spoons
1 small-medium onion, sliced	measuring cup
1/8 tsp. garlic powder	serving spoon
1/4 tsp. crushed red pepper flakes	
(or more, to taste)	
1 tsp. cornstarch	
3 tbsp. soy sauce	
2 tbsp. sherry	

1/2 6-oz. package frozen Chinese
   pea pods
1/4 c. dry roasted peanuts

Start rice.
   Cut pork into 1/2" cubes. Heat oil until hot in heavy skillet. Add pork. Brown, stirring occasionally for 2-4 minutes. Meanwhile mince ginger. Slice onion. Combine cornstarch, soy sauce, and sherry in measuring cup.
   Add onions to skillet, stir, and sauté 1 minute more. Add red pepper, ginger, and garlic powder. Stir 30 seconds. Add soy sauce mixture and stir. Add pea pods, stir, and cook 1 minute. Add peanuts, stir, and serve mixture over rice.

Time: 15 minutes
Serves: 2 generously

SWEET-AND-SOUR PORK

Serve it over rice and don't bother with another vegetable; this absolutely scrumptious dish is very rich and very filling. Can be made a day in advance.

INGREDIENTS	UTENSILS
2 boneless pork chops, cut into bite-sized pieces	large, heavy skillet with lid
1 egg	2 small mixing bowls
3 tbsp. vegetable oil	measuring spoons
1/2 c. flour	sharp knife
1½ tsp. salt	large plate
1/2 tsp. pepper	measuring cup
4 tbsp. butter	cutting board
1 small onion, sliced thin	mixing spoon
1 green pepper, core removed and shell cut into thin strips	2 forks
1 c. hot water	
1 chicken boullion cube	
1 8¼-oz. can sliced pineapple (cut up in can like pie slices) with juice	
1/8 tsp. garlic powder	
2 tbsp. soy sauce	
2 tbsp. lemon juice	
4 tbsp. wine vinegar	
1/3 c. packed dark brown sugar	
1 tbsp. cornstarch, dissolved in 1 tbsp. cold water	

Start rice according to directions for Parsley Rice (see Index), but omit the parsley.

Put 2 tbsp. each vegetable oil and butter into skillet over medium-high heat to melt while you beat lightly with fork 1 tbsp. vegetable oil and 1 egg in a small mixing bowl. In other bowl mix the flour, salt, and pepper. Cut pork into chunks, dip in egg and then flour. Put in skillet to brown, but do not let pieces touch each other. Continue to coat and cook pork, putting uncooked and cooked pieces as they are prepared on the large plate.*

While the last of the pork is cooking, cut up onion and green pepper. When pork is through, add 2 tbsp. butter to pan and onion and green pepper. Sauté lightly. Put hot water and boullion into measuring cup. Add to skillet along with pineapple chunks and juice, the garlic powder, and the pork pieces. Stir.

In measuring cup, measure sugar. Add soy sauce, lemon juice, and wine vinegar. Mix and add to skillet. Stir, cover, and cook on high heat 5-7 minutes. Add the cornstarch which has been dissolved in cold water. Stir until thickened and serve immediately over the rice.

Time: 25-30 minutes
Serves: 2 generously

*Cooked pork can be frozen if you wish to prepare the sauce at a later date.

SAUSAGE AND SAUCES

Cabbage is much overlooked and is especially good here with the strong taste of sausage. This dish should surprise and please you.

INGREDIENTS	UTENSILS
1 tbsp. bacon fat or vegetable oil	large, heavy skillet with lid
1 8-oz. package of precooked sausages	large, sharp knife large bowl
1 small head of cabbage (or half a larger head), sliced thin	vegetable peeler cutting board small saucepan
2 carrots, sliced thin	small serving bowl
1/4 tsp. salt	measuring spoons
1/2 c. cold applesauce	paper towel 2 forks
	mixing spoon
SAUCE	
1/2 pt. sour cream	
1 tsp. prepared horseradish	
1/4 tsp. salt	
1/8 tsp. cayenne pepper	

In heavy skillet brown the sausages in the bacon fat over medium-high heat. Meanwhile halve the cabbage and remove most of the hard center core. Then cut the cabbage into very thin slices and add to large bowl. Peel, slice carrots, and stir into bowl. Remove browned sausages to doubled paper towel, and sauté cabbage and carrots in the hot fat for 3 minutes.

Add the sausages and salt, reduce heat to low, cover, and simmer 10 minutes. Stir occasionally.

Meanwhile put all sauce ingredients in saucepan. Mix and let sit. During last 5 minutes heat slowly (do not boil or sour cream will curdle). Pour sauce into serving dish; serve cold applesauce on the side.

Time: sautéing: 5-8 minutes
       cooking: 10-15 minutes
Serves: 2

SAUSAGE-STUFFED TOMATOES

An attractive, delicious, and different way to serve sausage. Excellent for brunch.

INGREDIENTS	UTENSILS
1 tbsp. butter	heavy skillet
2 large tomatoes	bowl
1/2 lb. hot sausage meat	paring knife
1/2 c. bread crumbs	measuring cup
2 tbsp. garlic-flavored red wine vinegar or 2 tbsp. red wine vinegar and 1/8 tsp. garlic powder	measuring spoons
	mixing spoon
	8" baking dish
	cutting board
2 tbsp. onion, minced fine	
2 tbsp. fresh parsley, minced	
1/4 tsp. celery salt	
1/4 tsp. freshly ground black pepper	

Preheat oven to 350°. Grease baking dish with part of the 1 tbsp. butter.

Sauté sausage meat with remaining butter in skillet over medium heat. Halve tomatoes crosswise, scoop out centers and discard them. Put tomato halves into greased baking dish. Put all other ingredients into bowl and mix well. Add cooked sausage to mixture in bowl and blend well. Spoon mixture into tomato halves* and bake 5 minutes.

Time: sautéing: 15 minutes
       baking: 5 minutes
Serves: 2

*Can be made several hours in advance to this point. Bake until thoroughly warm.

SAUERKRAUT AND KNACKWURST IN VERMOUTH

Delicious served with boiled new potatoes and prepared spicy mustard.

INGREDIENTS
2 strips bacon, cut into 1" pieces
1 medium onion, sliced into 1/2"
  pieces
12 oz. Knackwurst or
  frankfurters
1 8-oz. can sauerkraut
1/2 c. vermouth
1 tart apple, cored and quartered

UTENSILS
large, heavy skillet
  or Dutch oven
can opener
paring knife
cutting board
measuring cup
mixing spoon
fork

Sauté bacon pieces in skillet over medium-high heat. Meanwhile prepare onion and apple. When bacon begins to brown, add onions and Knackwurst. Turn sausage as necessary. Sauté until onions are golden. Add sauerkraut and vermouth. Top with apples. Cover and cook on medium heat 15-20 minutes.

Time: sautéing: 10 minutes
       cooking: 15-20 minutes
Serves: 2

VEAL CHOPS SUPREME

Tender veal in an outstanding wine-and-cream sauce. Rice goes beautifully with this.

INGREDIENTS
1 tbsp. butter
2 loin veal chops or 1/2 lb. veal
  cutlets or veal steak
1/2 c. hot water
1 chicken boullion cube
2 tbsp. lemon juice
1 heaping tbsp. fresh parsley,
  minced
1/3 c. whipping cream
1 tbsp. dry sherry or brandy

UTENSILS
large, heavy skillet
  with lid
paring knife
measuring cup
measuring spoons
mixing spoon
plate
cutting board

Melt butter in skillet over medium-high heat. Add chops and sauté 3-5 minutes on each side. Meanwhile chop parsley. Measure water; add boullion cube and lemon juice to cup and mix. Add liquid to skillet; cover and cook 3 minutes on each side. Remove chops to plate. Turn heat to high and cook, uncovered, until liquid is reduced by half. Add parsley, cream, and sherry to skillet, scraping up pan brownings; stir thoroughly until sauce thickens. Return chops to skillet. Coat with sauce and serve.

Time: 16-20 minutes
Serves: 2

GRUYERE VEAL

This dish has everything: it's easy and fast to prepare—great to make in advance for a dinner party; it's absolutely delicious and a little bit different. Serve it over rice and start the rice before you begin the veal.

INGREDIENTS
1/2 lb. boneless veal, cut into
    4 pieces, or 2 boneless and
    skinless chicken breasts
salt
pepper
1/4 c. flour
3 tbsp. butter
4 green onions, sliced thin
1 3-oz. can mushrooms, drained,
    or 6-8 fresh mushrooms,
    wiped clean and sliced
1/3 c. dry white wine
1/3 c. whipping cream
2 oz. Gruyère cheese

UTENSILS
large, heavy skillet
cutting board
paring knife
measuring spoons
measuring cup
8" baking dish
2 forks or tongs
mixing spoon
cheese grater
waxed paper
mallet or rolling pin
can opener

Preheat oven to 400°.

Place veal between 2 slices of waxed paper and pound until approximately 1/4" thick. Salt, pepper, and lightly flour veal. Melt butter in skillet over medium-high heat. As soon as butter is bubbly, add veal and brown quickly on each side. Meanwhile prepare onions and mushrooms. Remove veal to baking dish. Add onions and mushrooms to skillet and sauté 1-2 minutes. Add wine and cream and cook 1 minute while stirring. Pour cream mixture over veal. Grate cheese over veal* and bake in oven 5 minutes.

Time: preparation and sautéing: 10 minutes
           baking: 5 minutes
Serves: 2

*Can be made a day in advance to this point or frozen.

TARRAGON VEAL

One of the simplest and most appetizing main dishes that we've ever sampled. Serve over Parsley Rice (see Index) and start rice before you begin to cook veal. Tarragon Veal can be prepared a day in advance, but you may have to add extra vermouth when you reheat it.

INGREDIENTS
1/2 lb. boneless veal, cut into 4
    pieces, or 2 boneless and
    skinless chicken breasts
2 green onions, sliced thin
1 3-oz. can mushrooms or 6-8 fresh
    mushrooms, cleaned and sliced
salt
white pepper
1/4 c. flour
1½ tbsp. vegetable oil
1½ tbsp. butter
1/2 c. dry vermouth or white wine
1½ tsp. fresh tarragon, chopped,
    or 3/4 tsp. dried tarragon

UTENSILS
large, heavy skillet
waxed paper
mallet or rolling pin
paring knife
cutting board
measuring spoons
measuring cup
mixing spoon
tongs or 2 forks
can opener

Place veal between 2 slices waxed paper and pound until approximately 1/4" thick. Salt, pepper, and lightly flour veal. Melt butter in skillet over medium-high heat while you prepare the onions and mushrooms. As soon as butter is bubbly, add veal and brown quickly on each side. Remove veal to waxed paper. Add onions and mushrooms to skillet and sauté 1-2 minutes. Stir in vermouth and tarragon. Return veal to skillet; cover, reduce heat to low, and simmer 5-6 minutes.

Time: 12-14 minutes
Serves: 2

FISH FILLETS POACHED IN WINE, AU GRATIN

Elegant and extremely delicious. The rich sauce makes the most of a small amount of fish and seems to appeal to just about everyone. For variety, try bay scallops in place of fish fillets and reduce cooking time to 5 minutes.

INGREDIENTS
1/2 lb. flounder or sole fillets,
    washed and dried
salt
pepper
1 tbsp. onion, minced fine
3 tbsp. butter
2/3 c. dry vermouth or white wine
1/4 c. water

UTENSILS
non-aluminum saucepan
ovenproof, flameproof
    casserole
measuring spoons
measuring cup
cheese grater
paring knife
mixing spoon

1½ tbsp. flour
1/4 c. whipping cream
1 tbsp. fresh parsley, minced
1/4 c. Swiss cheese, grated

waxed paper
cutting board
toothpicks
plate
4 paper towels

Preheat broiler. Chop onions and parsley. Wash and dry fish.

Season fillets with salt and pepper; roll and secure each with tooth-picks. In casserole layer onions and rolled fillets. Mix wine and water and pour over fish. Bring to simmer on top of stove. Cover with top or piece of waxed paper that has been buttered on side facing fish. Simmer 6-8 minutes or until tender.

Grate cheese. Remove rolled fillets to plate. Reduce fish liquid by half over high heat. Blend flour and remaining butter in saucepan over medium-high heat. Add fish liquid, cream, and parsley to saucepan. Stir constantly until thick and smooth. Pour sauce over the fish in casserole. Sprinkle cheese on top. Broil until lightly browned.

Time: 20 minutes
Serves: 2

SOLE IN HERB BUTTER

A tasty and unusual variation on broiled fish that can be ready to serve in less than 10 minutes.

INGREDIENTS
3/4 lb. fillets of sole or flounder*
5½ tbsp. butter
1/8 tsp. salt
1/8 tsp. onion powder
1/4 tsp. fresh parsley, minced
1/4 tsp. dried thyme
1 tbsp. Hellmann's mayonnaise
1 tbsp. lemon juice

UTENSILS
4 paper towels
medium flameproof
  dish
spatula
measuring spoons
small saucepan
mixing spoon
paring knife
cutting board

Preheat broiler to 550°. Butter baking dish with 1/2 tbsp. of the butter. Rinse fish fillets in cold water and dry between paper towels.

Melt butter in saucepan. Mince parsley; stir it and remaining ingredients into butter. Place fish in baking dish and top with the butter sauce. Broil 3-4 inches from heat for 3 minutes. Baste fillets and broil 1 minute. Serve immediately.

Time: 8-10 minutes
Serves: 2

*Although fresh fish is always preferable, even frozen fillets can be quite tasty when prepared in this manner. If you haven't remembered to thaw the fish, place unopened package in hot water for 15-20 minutes.

CURRIED SALMON CAKES
WITH WHITE SAUCE

The perfect main dish when you haven't had time to shop. You may substitute tuna packed in water.

INGREDIENTS
1 7-oz. can salmon, drained
1/3 c. bread crumbs
2 tbsp. fresh parsley, minced
1 tbsp. minced onion
1 tsp. celery salt
1/4 tsp. pepper
1 tsp. curry powder
2 eggs
2 tbsp. butter
2 tbsp. oil

WHITE SAUCE
2 tbsp. butter
1 tbsp. flour
1/4 tsp. salt
1/8 tsp. pepper
1/3 c. milk

UTENSILS
large skillet
small saucepan
fork
mixing spoon
metal spatula
medium bowl
measuring spoons
measuring cup
cutting board
paring knife
can opener
large plate

Mince parsley and onion; add to mixing bowl along with bread crumbs, celery salt, pepper, curry powder, and 2 eggs. Mix well with fork. Clean salmon with paring knife over large plate. Add salmon to bowl, crumble into tiny bits, and mix well with fork. Form mixture into 4 cakes. Heat butter and oil in skillet over high heat until bubbly. Reduce heat to medium, add cakes, and brown 3 minutes. Turn cakes and brown 3-4 minutes.

Meanwhile melt butter in saucepan over medium-high heat. Add flour, salt, and pepper; blend. Add milk and stir constantly until well blended and thickened. Serve over salmon cakes.

Time: preparation: 5 minutes
          cooking: 6-7 minutes
Serves: 2 very generously

SCALLOPS A LA NEWBURG

If you don't have scallops, use thawed crab meat or, if desperate, canned tuna in water. Decide if you wish to serve the scallops over rice (see Index), patty shells, or toast points and start them as necessary.

INGREDIENTS
2 tbsp. butter
1/2 lb. bay scallops (or halved sea
    scallops)

UTENSILS
paring knife
2 paper towels
medium-sized non-

2 tsp. flour	aluminum skillet
1/4 tsp. paprika	with top
1/4 tsp. salt	measuring spoons
1/8 tsp. nutmeg	serving spoon
1/4 c. dry sherry	measuring cup
1/2 c. whipping cream	fork
2 egg yolks	cutting board
1 tbsp. fresh parsley, minced	
1 tbsp. Cognac or brandy	

Melt butter in skillet over medium heat; do not let brown. Wash scallops and dry on paper towels. Add to skillet and swirl in butter. Add flour, paprika, salt, and nutmeg, and stir. Add dry sherry and stir. Cover and cook for 5-10 minutes, depending on size of scallops. Meanwhile mince parsley. Measure cream in pitcher, add egg yolks, and mix well with fork. Stir cream mixture into skillet and stir constantly until thickened; do not boil or sauce will curdle. Add minced parsley and brandy. Cook 30 seconds more and serve.

Time: 15 minutes
Serves: 2

SHRIMP SAUTE

Simply delicious, and best served over rice (see Index). An easy clear-cut recipe that takes the mystery out of preparing fresh shrimp.

INGREDIENTS	UTENSILS
1/2 lb. raw, unshelled jumbo	large, heavy skillet
shrimp	cutting board
4 tbsp. butter	paring knife
1/4 c. chives, chopped	measuring cup
1/4 c. fresh parsley, chopped	measuring spoons
1/8-1/4 tsp. garlic powder	2 forks, spoons, or
1/2 c. dry white wine	tongs
1 tsp. Kikoman soy sauce	2 paper towels

Wash shrimp and peel off shell with fingers (you may leave tail on for a more dramatic effect). Make a shallow cut lengthwise down back of each shrimp; wash out sand vein. Dry well on paper towels.

Melt butter in skillet over high heat. Meanwhile chop parsley and chives. When butter is bubbly and very hot (but not burning), instantly add shrimp and sauté 2 minutes on each side. Add garlic, parsley, and chives. Stir. Stir in wine and soy sauce, scraping brownings from skillet. Cook 3 minutes and serve.

Time: preparation: 5 minutes
       cooking: 10 minutes
Serves: 2

SHRIMP CREOLE

A superbly subtle sauce envelopes and masks the frozen shrimp in a very filling entrée when it is served over rice, which should, of course, be started before the creole (see Index). For a truer creole that would serve more than two, add cooked ham or chicken chunks. Or for a variation, substitute sliced boneless chicken breast for the shrimp, and sauté the meat along with the peppers and onion.

INGREDIENTS
3 tbsp. butter
1 medium onion, chopped
1 small green pepper, cored and
    chopped
2 c. fresh tomatoes, chopped, or
    1 16-oz. can tomatoes with
    juice
1 bay leaf
1/8 tsp. garlic powder
1/8 tsp. pepper
3/4 tsp. salt
1/4 tsp. Worcestershire sauce
2 dashes Tobasco sauce
1/2 c. dry white wine

1 tbsp. water
1 tbsp. cornstarch
1 8-oz. package small, frozen,
    precooked shrimp

UTENSILS
paring knife
cutting board
mixing spoon
large, heavy skillet
measuring spoons
measuring cup
can opener
strainer

Melt butter in skillet over medium-high heat while you chop the pepper, onion, and fresh tomatoes. Turn heat to high, add vegetables, and sauté 5 minutes, stirring occasionally. Add bay leaf, garlic, salt, pepper, Worcestershire sauce, Tobasco, and wine. (If you are using undrained canned tomatoes, crush tomatoes with spoon against the side of the can and add tomatoes and juice at this point.) Stir, reduce heat to low, cover, and cook 5 minutes.

Meanwhile pick over shrimp and rinse them in strainer until thawed. Blend cornstarch and water in measuring cup. Add shrimp to skillet. Stir. Stir in cornstarch mixture and stir constantly until sauce thickens. Serve immediately over rice.

Time: 18-20 minutes
Serves: 2 very generously

SHRIMP FONDUE

Everyone thinks shrimp is a special treat. Our fast and inexpensive fondue captures that delicious flavor in a rich and creamy sauce which goes equally well with bread cubes, toast, or vegetables. If you can't be bothered with the fondue process, simply heat the sauce and serve it over toast points.

INGREDIENTS
1 10¾-oz. Campbell's Cream of
    Shrimp Soup
1 8-oz. package cream cheese
1 4¼-oz. can tiny shrimp
1 tsp. lemon juice
1 tsp. Worcestershire sauce
1/4 c. sour cream
1 tbsp. brandy
2 tbsp. chopped green onions or
    chives
2 tbsp. minced parsley

UTENSILS
fondue pot or 1-qt.
    saucepan
can opener
rubber spatula
measuring spoons
paring knife
cutting board
wire whisk

Over medium heat start to blend shrimp soup, cream cheese, shrimp, lemon juice, and Worcestershire sauce. Meanwhile chop green onions and parsley and add to pot. Add brandy and sour cream and whisk until smooth and hot. Do not boil or sauce will curdle! Transfer pot to fondue stand or serve sauce over toast points.

Time: preparation: 3-5 minutes
        cooking: 10 minutes
Makes: 3 cups

VEGETABLES

FRESH ASPARAGUS

Asparagus prepared in this manner is certainly one of the most delicious dishes you may encounter. As the supreme variation, omit the lemon butter and top with Hollandaise sauce (see Index).

INGREDIENTS
16 stalks fresh asparagus
1 tsp. salt
1 qt. water
2 tbsp. butter
1 tsp. lemon juice

UTENSILS
12" skillet with lid
paring knife
measuring spoons
butter melter or small
    pot
cutting board
mixing spoon
slotted metal spatula
2 serving plates

Pour water into skillet and put on high heat. Meanwhile cut 1/8" off bottom of each asparagus stalk and lift off scales with paring knife. Lightly scrape outer skin from last 2" at bottom of stalks (or where color is not green). Discard scrapings, etc., and wash stalks. Cut bottoms off stalks to make all tops about 8" long. Put tops into skillet and cut bottoms into 1/8" slices. Add these to the skillet and cook for 10 minutes. Cover and cook 5 minutes more.

Meanwhile melt butter in butter melter and stir in lemon juice. Lift out asparagus stalks with spatula and arrange on serving plates. (Reserve and refrigerate liquid and cooked slices for soup at a later date. See Index for Cream of Fresh Asparagus Soup.) Pour lemon butter over stalks and serve.

Time: 20 minutes
Serves: 2

CRANBERRY-ORANGE BEETS

Tangy, fruity, and a little spicy. Certainly delicious and easy to fix.

INGREDIENTS
1 8-oz. can sliced beets, drained
1/3 c. cranberry-orange relish
1 tsp. lemon juice

UTENSILS
small saucepan with
    lid
measuring cup
measuring spoon
mixing spoon

Mix all ingredients in saucepan over high heat. Stir and bring to a boil. Reduce heat to low, cover, and simmer 3 minutes.

Time: 5 minutes
Serves: 2

CREAMED BEANS

Until you taste this, you'll never guess how absolutely delicious it is.

INGREDIENTS
1/4 c. dry white wine or vermouth
3/4 tsp. salt
1/2 9-oz. package frozen French-
    cut string beans*
1/4 c. whipping cream
1/2 tsp. dry mustard dissolved in
    1 tsp. water
1 tbsp. butter
1 tbsp. sliced almonds

UTENSILS
small saucepan with lid
measuring cup
measuring spoons
mixing spoon
fork

Put salt and white wine in saucepan and bring to boil over high heat. Add string beans and break beans apart with fork. Bring to second boil, cover, and cook over medium-high heat for 5-6 minutes or until liquid has gone.

Meanwhile add the dissolved mustard to the cream in the measuring cup. Add cream mixture, butter, and almonds to cooked beans. Mix and cook 3 minutes. Remove from heat. Stir and cover until ready to serve.

Time: 14 minutes
Serves: 2

SWEET-AND-SOUR STRING BEANS

A different and most tasty way to serve green beans.

INGREDIENTS
1 tbsp. bacon fat or butter
1 small green onion or 1 tiny
    yellow onion, sliced thin
1/4 c. water
1/8 tsp. black pepper
1/4 tsp. salt
2 tsp. brown sugar
1½ tsp. wine vinegar
1/2 9-oz. package frozen string beans*

UTENSILS
small saucepan with
    lid
measuring spoons
measuring cup
mixing spoon
fork
paring knife
cutting board

Melt bacon fat in saucepan over medium-high heat while you slice the onion. Sauté onion, salt, and pepper 1 minute. Add water. Turn heat to high and add brown sugar. Stir and bring to boil. Add beans and break them apart with fork. Bring to boil again; reduce to medium heat, cover, and cook 6 minutes. Add wine vinegar and stir. Bring to boil. Stir, drain.

Time: 12 minutes
Serves: 2

*It's very easy to cut the entire frozen package in half with a large scalloped knife. Then take the empty container half and top the full half, which should be returned to freezer for later use.

BEETS AND WHITE GRAPES

A most attractive and refreshing side dish.

INGREDIENTS
1 8-oz. can sliced beets, with
    1/2 of the liquid drained
10 white grapes, split (or 1/4 c.
    white raisins)
1 tbsp. butter
1/2 tsp. grated lemon rind
1/4 tsp. sugar
1 tsp. cornstarch, dissolved in
    2 tsp. cold water

UTENSILS
small saucepan with
    cover
paring knife
measuring spoons
mixing spoon

Split grapes. Put first 5 ingredients in saucepan over high heat. Stir and bring to a boil. Reduce heat to low, cover, and simmer 3 minutes. Add cornstarch mixture and stir until smooth and thickened. Serve.

Time: 6 minutes
Serves: 2

BRAISED BRUSSEL SPROUTS

A much neglected vegetable, very tastily prepared here—thanks to the boullion, which cuts the strong flavor and permits a most subtle sprout to emerge.

INGREDIENTS
1/2 c. water
1/2 beef boullion cube
1/4 tsp. celery salt
1/4 tsp. sugar
1/8 tsp. pepper
1 10-oz. package frozen Brussel
    sprouts
1 tbsp. butter
1 tsp. lemon juice
1 tbsp. fresh parsley, minced

UTENSILS
1-qt. saucepan with lid
measuring cup
measuring spoons
paring knife
mixing spoon
cutting board

Put first 5 ingredients in saucepan and bring to a boil over high heat. Stir, then add sprouts and break apart with spoon. Cover and cook over medium-high heat 10 minutes until liquid is absorbed. Add remaining ingredients, shaking pan until butter is melted and sprouts are well coated.

Time: 15 minutes
Serves: 2 generously

BROCCOLI WITH LEMON CRUMBS

*An amazingly simple and delicious way to rescue frozen broccoli.**

INGREDIENTS
1 10-oz. package frozen broccoli
4 tbsp. butter
2 tsp. lemon juice
2 tbsp. bread crumbs

UTENSILS
medium saucepan with
   lid
butter melter or small
   saucepan
measuring cup
measuring spoon
mixing spoon

Cook broccoli according to package instructions. Meanwhile melt butter in small saucepan over medium-high heat; add bread crumbs and sauté 1-2 minutes; add lemon juice and stir. Drain broccoli with pot lid. Place broccoli on dinner plates, sprinkle lemon crumbs over top, and serve.

Time: 12 minutes
Serves: 2 generously

*If you have the time, use fresh broccoli. Bring 2 c. water and 1/2 tsp. salt to a boil in a large saucepan. Wash, cut off bottom 1/2" of stalks, and peel off tough outer skin of stalks. Cut head into small florets; cut stalks and stems into bite-size pieces. Place in boiling water. Cover and cook until water comes again to a boil (2-3 minutes). Uncover and cook 3 minutes or until crisply tender. Drain and serve.

CREAMY BRUSSEL SPROUTS

Sour cream and mustard provide a different and delicious sauce.

INGREDIENTS
1 c. hot water
5/8 tsp. salt
1 10-oz. package frozen Brussel
  sprouts
2 tbsp. butter
4 tbsp. sour cream
1/8 tsp. dry mustard
1/8 tsp. white pepper

UTENSILS
1-qt. saucepan with lid
measuring cup
measuring spoons
mixing spoon
small bowl

Put 1 c. hot water and 1/2 tsp. salt in saucepan over high heat. Bring to boil and add Brussel sprouts. Bring to second boil. Break sprouts apart with spoon. Cover and cook 10 minutes. Drain with lid. Remove sprouts to bowl.

In saucepan on low heat melt butter. Add 1/8 tsp. each salt, pepper, mustard; add sour cream, stirring until well blended. Return sprouts to saucepan. Heat 1 minute and serve.

Time: 18 minutes
Serves: 2 generously

CREAMED CABBAGE

This is not your standard boring, mushy cabbage. The cooking method and sauce combine to make a most surprisingly delightful dish.

INGREDIENTS
3 tbsp. bacon fat*
1/2 head small green cabbage
1/2 tsp. salt
1/4 tsp. white pepper
2 tbsp. flour
3/4 tsp. onion powder
1/3 c. milk

UTENSILS
large, heavy skillet
  with lid
large, sharp knife
measuring spoons
measuring cup
mixing spoon
cutting board

Melt bacon fat in heavy skillet over medium-high heat. Slice cabbage thin, removing bulk of center core. Add to skillet and sauté 5 minutes. Add salt, pepper, and onion powder. Cover and reduce heat to medium. Cook 5 more minutes. Add flour and stir well. Pour in milk and stir constantly until thick and smooth.

Time: 15 minutes
Serves: 2

* 3 tbsp. butter may be substituted, but this will give the dish a different flavor. If you do use butter, melt at medium heat or butter will burn.

CREAMED CARROTS

The cream cheese makes a light yet full-bodied sauce that enhances the flavor of the carrots.

INGREDIENTS
1/2 c. water
1/4 tsp. salt
4 good-sized carrots, peeled and
    cut in 1x1/4" strips
1 tbsp. butter
1/8 tsp. white pepper
1/4 tsp. celery salt
1 oz. cream cheese
1 tbsp. chopped chives

UTENSILS
medium saucepan with
    lid
measuring cup
measuring spoons
vegetable peeler
paring knife
mixing spoon
cutting board

Bring water and salt to a boil over high heat. Meanwhile peel and slice carrots. Add carrots to pan and bring to a second boil. Cover and cook on low heat for 10 minutes. Chop chives. Drain any excess water. Add remaining ingredients and stir gently until well blended.

Time: 18 minutes
Serves: 2

MAPLE-GINGER CARROTS

The ingredients are simple, but the taste is unusually tangy and delicious.

INGREDIENTS
1/4 c. water
1/4 tsp. salt
2 medium-to-large carrots, peeled
    and cut into 1/8" slices
1 tbsp. butter
1/4 tsp. ground ginger
1/2 tsp. lemon juice
1 tbsp. maple syrup

UTENSILS
small saucepan with
    cover
measuring cup
measuring spoons
mixing spoon
vegetable peeler
paring knife
cutting board

Put water and salt into saucepan over high heat. Meanwhile peel and slice carrots. Add carrots, cover, and boil on high heat for 5-7 minutes or until water evaporates. Watch carefully during last few minutes so that carrots do not burn. Add butter, ground ginger, lemon juice, and maple syrup; stir. Remove from heat and cover. Stir before serving.

Time: 10 minutes
Serves: 2

THREE C'S

Carrots, celery, and cheese combine to make a really good side dish.

INGREDIENTS
1/2 c. hot water
1 chicken boullion cube
3 medium carrots, peeled and cut
    into 1/8" slices
1 large stalk celery, cut into
    1/8" slices
1 tbsp. butter
1½ tbsp. flour
1/8 tsp. salt
1/8 tsp. white pepper
1/3 c. milk
1 1" square Cheddar cheese
1 tsp. lemon juice

UTENSILS
1-qt. saucepan with
    lid
measuring cup
measuring spoons
mixing spoon
vegetable peeler
paring knife
cutting board

Bring water and boullion cube to a boil in saucepan over high heat. Meanwhile peel, wash, and slice carrots 1/8" thick. Add to saucepan. Wash and slice celery into 1/8" pieces and add to pan. Cover and boil 5 minutes or until liquid is absorbed. Cut up cheese while carrots and celery are boiling. Remove saucepan from heat; add butter and stir gently until butter melts. Stir in salt, pepper, and flour and blend well. Add milk and stir constantly over high heat until mixture is thick and smooth. Add cheese and lemon juice and stir until well blended.

Time: 15 minutes
Serves: 2

BROILED CAULIFLOWER

Spectacular in appearance and taste.

INGREDIENTS
1½ c. water
1/2 tsp. salt
1/2 medium cauliflower
3 tbsp. Hellmann's mayonnaise
1/2 c. grated Cheddar cheese

UTENSILS
2-qt. saucepan with lid
small baking dish
measuring cup
measuring spoons
cheese grater
slotted spoon

Put water and salt in saucepan over high heat and bring to a boil. Meanwhile remove outer leaves and wash cauliflower. Add cauliflower to pot, cover, and boil 15 minutes. Preheat broiler. Grate cheese.

Remove cauliflower to baking dish with slotted spoon. Mix mayonnaise and cheese in measuring cup and spread mixture over the outer surface of the cauliflower.* Broil 4" from heat for 3-5 minutes or until golden brown.

Time: 20-25 minutes
Serves 2

*Can be made several hours in advance to this point; then reheat by baking at 400° 10-15 minutes or until cauliflower is hot and cheese is golden.

CURRIED CELERY AND APPLES

An unusual and refreshing combination of ingredients.

INGREDIENTS
3 tbsp. butter
1 small onion, sliced thin
1 large stalk celery, with leaves,
    sliced diagonally 1/8" thick
1 apple, peeled, quartered, cored,
    and sliced 1/8" thick
1/4 tsp. salt
1/8 tsp. freshly ground black
    pepper
1/4 tsp. curry powder, dissolved
    in 1/2 tbsp. water

UTENSILS
small skillet with lid
paring knife
measuring spoons
mixing spoon
cutting board

Melt butter in skillet over medium heat. Meanwhile slice onion and celery. Sauté onion until translucent. Add celery. Cover and cook for 5-7 minutes (until just tender). Meanwhile slice apples, add to skillet, cover, and cook 3 minutes. Add other ingredients and stir over heat for 1 minute.

Time: 15 minutes
Serves: 2

SAUTEED LETTUCE

Few people have ever tasted, much less enjoyed, cooked lettuce. It can be surprisingly delicious, as our recipe proves, and also an excellent way to use up wilted or bolted lettuce. For extra flavors and colors, add 1 tbsp. of your favorite fresh herb.

INGREDIENTS
2 c. iceberg, Romaine, or escarole
   lettuce, shredded
1 tbsp. vegetable oil
1/8 tsp. white pepper
1/8 tsp. garlic powder
1/4 tsp. salt

UTENSILS
large, sharp knife
cutting board
colander or large
   strainer
mixing spoon
measuring spoons
large, heavy skillet

Wash lettuce, drain, and cut into thin strips. Just before serving, heat oil, salt, pepper, and garlic powder in skillet over medium-high heat. When oil is just hot but not smoking, add lettuce and stir 30-60 seconds.

Time: preparation: 3 minutes
        cooking: 1-1½ minutes
Serves: 2

ONIONS ALMONDINE

Those who love onions will be delighted with this as a main vegetable or as a topping for hamburgers or other meat. Those who do not adore those odiferous orbs will be pleased by the subtle flavor the vermouth seems to induce.

INGREDIENTS
2 medium-large onions
2 tbsp. butter
1/4 c. almonds
1/4 c. dry vermouth or dry white
   wine

UTENSILS
medium skillet with lid
sharp knife
mixing spoon
cutting board
measuring cup

While butter is melting in skillet over medium-high heat, peel onions and halve and slice them into 1/8" sections. Add onions to skillet as sliced and sauté 5 minutes, stirring occasionally. Add almonds and sauté 1 minute. Add vermouth, stir, cover, and cook 5 minutes. Stir and serve.

Time: 14 minutes
Serves: 2

THE BEST CREAMED ONIONS EVER

If you love onions, you'll sigh over this deliciously rich and creamy dish.

INGREDIENTS	UTENSILS
1/2 lb. small white onions	paring knife
1 chicken boullion cube	1-qt. saucepan with top
2 c. water	mixing spoon
1/8 tsp. salt	measuring spoons
pinch white pepper	1-qt. pitcher
1 tbsp. butter	slotted spoon
1 tbsp. Wondra granulated flour	
2 tbsp. whipping cream	

Put water on to boil while you peel the onions. Add chicken boullion cube to water, mash with spoon, and stir. Put onions 3/4-1" in diameter in saucepan.Bring to boil and cook over high heat 2 minutes. Add smaller onions, bring to boil. Reduce heat to low, cover, and cook 5 minutes. Remove onions and juice to pitcher. Melt butter and white pepper and salt over medium heat. Add flour and stir well. Remove from heat and stir in scant 1/4 c. onion liquid and 2 tbsp. cream. Stir constantly over high heat until thickened. Remove onions with slotted spoon to saucepan. Gently turn onions about in sauce.

Time: 15 minutes
Serves: 2

MINT PEAS

A great summertime treat . . . delicious whenever fresh mint is available.

INGREDIENTS	UTENSILS
1 tbsp. butter	small saucepan with
1/4 tsp. salt	lid
1/8 tsp. freshly ground pepper	measuring spoons
1/2 10-oz. package frozen petite	paring knife
peas*	mixing spoon
20 mint leaves, sliced**	cutting board
1 tsp. tarragon vinegar	

Put butter, salt, and pepper in saucepan over medium heat while you wash and slice mint. Stir mint into melted butter. Add peas and break apart with fork. Stir, cover, and cook 3 minutes. Add vinegar, stir, and serve.

Time: 6 minutes
Serves: 2

*If you use regular green peas, add 1 tbsp. water and increase cooking time to 5 minutes.

**If you cannot find fresh mint, substitute 1/8 tsp. dried tarragon. Dried mint just doesn't measure up.

PIZZA PEAS

For variety, substitute sliced, pitted black olives for the green. They pro-vide a more subtle taste and look quite pretty.

INGREDIENTS
1 tbsp. butter
1/4 tsp. salt
1/4 tsp. dried oregano
1/8 tsp. freshly ground black
pepper
1/2 10-oz. package frozen petite
peas*
16 small, stuffed green olives,
sliced

UTENSILS
small saucepan with
lid
measuring spoons
mixing spoon
paring knife
cutting board

Put butter, salt, pepper, and oregano into saucepan over medium heat. Meanwhile slice olives. When butter is bubbly, add peas and break apart with spoon. Add olives to pan. Cover and cook 3 minutes. Stir and serve.

Time: 6 minutes
Serves: 2

*If you use regular peas, add 1 tbsp. water and increase cooking time to 5 minutes.

BROILED POTATO CHIPS

Speedy and delicious. A cross between French fries and potato chips. Top with a dollop of sour cream or Horseradish Sauce (see Index) for variety.

INGREDIENTS
2 medium Idaho potatoes,
unpeeled and washed
3 tbsp. butter
salt
pepper

UTENSILS
paring knife
cookie sheet
pastry brush or spoon
metal spatula
butter melter or small
saucepan

Preheat broiler.
Melt butter over low heat. Meanwhile cut potatoes into 1/8″ slices. Brush cookie sheet with 1 tbsp. of the melted butter. Arrange potato slices on cookie sheet. Do not overlap. Brush potatoes with remaining butter.
Place cookie sheet approximately 6″ from broiler and broil for 5 minutes. Turn slices with spatula and broil for 1½-2 minutes more or until golden brown. Sprinkle with salt and pepper before serving.

Time: 12 minutes
Serves: 2

DIJON POTATOES

The ultimate creamed potato: simple, quick, absolutely scrumptuous, and a little less fattening because there's no flour in the sauce.

INGREDIENTS
2-3 medium Idaho potatoes,
  peeled, halved, and cut into
  1/8" slices
2 c. water
1 tsp. salt
1 tsp. Dijon mustard
1/8 tsp. white pepper
3 tbsp. milk
1/2 c. grated Cheddar cheese
1 tbsp. fresh parsley, minced

UTENSILS
2-qt. saucepan with lid
measuring cup
measuring spoons
paring knife
cheese grater
mixing spoon
cutting board

Put water, salt, and pepper on to boil over high heat. Meanwhile peel and slice the potatoes, adding slices of each potato as you finish it. Stir, cover, and bring to boil. Reduce heat to medium-high and cook 10 minutes. Stir once after 5 minutes. Mince parsley and grate cheese. When potatoes are cooked, remove from heat and drain with lid. Add cheese and parsley and stir. Mix milk and mustard in measuring cup. Add to pot, stir, cover, and let sit 3 minutes. Stir well and serve.

Time: 23 minutes
Serves: 2

NEW POTATOES IN SOUR CREAM

The taste of baked potatoes with sour cream in one-fourth the time.

INGREDIENTS
4 tbsp. butter
6 small new potatoes, unpeeled,
  washed, and sliced
1/8 tsp. freshly ground pepper
1/2 tsp. salt
1/3 c. sour cream
1 tbsp. chopped chives

UTENSILS
large, heavy skillet
  with lid
paring knife
measuring spoons
measuring cup
mixing spoon
cutting board

Melt butter in skillet over medium heat. Slice potatoes and add to skillet. Add salt and pepper. Stir, cover, and cook on low heat for 10 minutes or until tender, stirring occasionally. Add sour cream and chives. Stir and heat 1 more minute. Do not boil or cream will curdle. Serve.

Time: 15 minutes
Serves: 2

SKILLET POTATOES

Lyonnaise potatoes with a delicious difference.

INGREDIENTS
3 tbsp. butter
2 medium Idaho potatoes,
   unpeeled and washed
1 medium onion
1/4 tsp. salt
1/8 tsp. freshly ground black
   pepper
1 c. beef stock or 1 beef boullion
   cube dissolved in 1 c. hot
   water
1 bay leaf
1 tbsp. fresh parsley, minced

UTENSILS
large, heavy skillet
   with lid
paring knife
measuring cup
measuring spoons
mixing spoon
cutting board

Melt butter in skillet over medium heat while you slice the potatoes very thin. Add them to the skillet as you slice them. Sauté the potatoes as you slice the onions thin. Add onions to the skillet, and sauté all for 5 minutes. Meanwhile mince parsley. Add all remaining ingredients. Stir, cover, and cook on high heat for 7 minutes or until potatoes are tender and liquid has been pretty much absorbed. Remove bay leaf. Stir and cover until ready to serve.

Time: 15 minutes
Serves: 2

BULGUR PILAF

Serve this hearty, delicious side dish instead of rice or potatoes for a pleasant change.

INGREDIENTS
2 tsp. butter
1/4 c. sliced celery
1/4 c. chopped onion
1/4 c. bulgur
1/2 c. water
1 boullion cube (chicken or beef)

UTENSILS
small skillet with cover
measuring cup
cutting board
paring knife
mixing spoon

Cut onion and celery. Melt butter in skillet over medium-high heat. Add celery and onion and sauté 2 minutes. Add bulgur and sauté an additional 2 minutes. Add water and boullion cube. Stir until cube dissolves. Cover and reduce heat to low. Cook 12 minutes or until broth is absorbed.

Time: 20 minutes
Serves: 2

PARSLEY RICE

Even if you are addicted to your present method of cooking rice, you should try ours once: this method is fast and absolutely never-fail, and the taste is so totally delicious that this rice stands on its own.

INGREDIENTS
1/2 c. long-grained rice
1 c. water
1 tbsp. butter
1 chicken or beef boullion cube
1/2 tsp. salt
1/4 tsp. pepper
1 tbsp. fresh parsley,* minced

UTENSILS
medium saucepan
  with lid
measuring spoons
measuring cup
fork
paring knife
cutting board

Combine all ingredients except parsley in saucepan and bring to a boil over high heat. Mix thoroughly with fork, cover, and reduce heat to low. Cook for 13 minutes; then remove from heat. Meanwhile mince parsley. Stir in parsley and cover until ready to serve.

Time: preparation: 2 minutes
        cooking: 13 minutes
Serves: 2

*You can use any fresh herbs (oregano, thyme, sage, rosemary, chives) or up to 1/2 c. shredded chicory, Romaine, or other lettuce for a different look and taste.

HERBED BROWN RICE

This is a double recipe since the rice is equally good hot or at room temperature. Allowing the rice to warm up a bit from refrigerator temperature removes an excess of crunchiness from this pretty, tasty, and healthy side dish. If you add a lot of chopped parsley, watercress, or fresh herbs, you eliminate the need for a green vegetable.

INGREDIENTS
1 c. brown rice
3 c. hot water
2 beef boullion cubes
1 tsp. salt
1/4 tsp. freshly ground black
  pepper
1/4 c. fresh chives or green
  onions, chopped
1 c. fresh parsley, chopped

UTENSILS
1½-qt. heavy saucepan
  with lid
strainer
measuring cup
measuring spoons
paring knife
cutting board
fork
3 paper towels

Bring hot water, salt, pepper, and boullion cubes to boil over high heat while you wash rice in strainer under hot water. Add rice, but do not stir and do not cover. Boil 15 minutes while you wash, dry, and chop parsley and chives.

When rice water just bubbles through the top of the rice, stir once, cover, and reduce heat to as low as possible. Cook 7 minutes or until water is absorbed. Add parsley and chives, stir, and serve half the portion the first night either warm or at room temperature. Refrigerate the remaining half and serve another night.

Time: 30 minutes
Serves: 4

CREAMED SPINACH

Cream cheese is the "secret ingredient" that makes this the easiest and tastiest creamed spinach you've ever tried.

INGREDIENTS
2 tbsp. butter
1 small onion, minced
1 10-oz. package frozen chopped
    spinach
1 3-oz. package cream cheese
1/2 tsp. salt
1/8 tsp. freshly ground pepper
1/8 tsp. ground nutmeg
1/8 tsp. garlic powder
1 tsp. fresh sage, minced,
    or 1/4 tsp. dried

UTENSILS
small skillet with lid
measuring spoons
fork
mixing spoon
paring knife
cutting board

Chop onion while butter melts in skillet over medium-high heat. When butter is bubbly, add onion and sauté about 30 seconds. Mince sage. Add spinach, cover, and cook 5 minutes. Break spinach apart with fork. Recover and cook 3-5 minutes more or until liquid has evaporated. Add remaining ingredients and stir until smooth, blended, and bubbly. Serve.

Time: 15 minutes
Serves: 2 generously

SPINACH PARMESAN

Cheese and just a touch of onion work wonders with frozen spinach.

INGREDIENTS
2 tbsp. butter
1/4 tsp. salt
1/2 tsp. onion powder
1 10-oz. package frozen leaf
  spinach
3 tbsp. grated Parmesan cheese

UTENSILS
1-qt. saucepan with lid
fork
measuring spoons
mixing spoon

Melt butter, salt, and onion powder in saucepan over medium-high heat. Add spinach, cover, and cook 5 minutes. Remove cover. Break up spinach with fork. Recover and cook 3 minutes on high heat or until liquid is evaporated. Sprinkle cheese over spinach just before serving.

Time: 12 minutes
Serves: 2

TOMATOES AND CROUTONS

Even anemic winter tomatoes are taste sensations when cooked in this manner.

INGREDIENTS
3 tbsp. butter
2 slices bread, cut in 1/4" cubes
2-3 large tomatoes, red or green*,
  cut in 1" cubes
1 tbsp. fresh parsley, minced
1 green onion, sliced thin
1/2 tsp. salt
1/8 tsp. black pepper
1/4 tsp. dried basil

UTENSILS
large, heavy skillet
  with lid
measuring spoons
paring knife
cutting board
small bowl
mixing spoon

Melt 2 tbsp. butter in skillet over medium heat. Meanwhile cube bread. Add bread cubes and sauté until golden brown. Cut up tomatoes, onions, and parsley. Remove sautéed croutons to a bowl. Add remaining butter to skillet and sauté onion lightly. Add herbs and spices; stir. Cover and cook 3-5 minutes on high heat, depending on the ripeness of the tomatoes (the riper the tomato, the shorter the cooking time). When ready to serve, remove any excess liquid with a spoon and stir in croutons.

Time: 13-15 minutes
Serves: 2

*The riper the tomato, the less bulk it has when cooked.

TURNIPS AU GRATIN

We think this dish will amaze you: it's pretty, it's delicious, it's very unusual, and it's turnip! Even turnip-haters will eat it willingly and be surprised when they find out the ingredients.

INGREDIENTS
2 tbsp. butter
2 large white turnips (approx.
   2 c. sliced)
1/2 tsp. salt
1/8 tsp. white pepper
1/4 tsp. sugar
1/2 c. water
1 tbsp. fresh thyme or oregano
   or parsley, minced
1 1-oz. wedge Gruyère cheese

UTENSILS
paring knife
cutting board
measuring spoons
6½-8" flameproof,
   ovenproof casserole
   with lid
cheese grater
mixing spoon

Wash and peel turnip. Halve turnips and cut into 1/8" slices. Put butter in flameproof pot over high heat. Add turnips to melted butter when sliced. Add salt, pepper, sugar, and water to pot. Stir, cover, and cook 3 minutes. Preheat broiler. Meanwhile mince the herb; grate cheese onto cutting board. Add herb to pot, stir, cover again, and cook 4-5 minutes or until liquid is absorbed. Remove from heat, uncover, stir, sprinkle grated cheese on top. Put under broiler for 1-2 minutes or until cheese begins to brown. Remove and serve.

Time: 13 minutes
Serves: 2

TURNIPS LYONNAISE

So good, you'll like them even if you've never cared for turnips before.

INGREDIENTS
3 tbsp. butter
2 large white turnips* (approx.
   2 c. sliced)
1 small onion
1/2 tsp. salt
1/8 tsp. freshly ground black
   pepper
1/2 tsp. lemon juice
1/2 c. water
1 tbsp. fresh parsley, minced

UTENSILS
small skillet with lid
measuring spoons
measuring cup
cutting board
paring knife
mixing spoon

Melt butter in skillet over medium-high heat. Peel turnips and onion, cut them in half, and then into 1/8" slices, adding to skillet as you slice. Sauté 2-3 minutes. Add all remaining ingredients except parsley; cover and cook 8 minutes or until liquid is absorbed. Chop parsley; garnish when ready to serve.

Time: 14 minutes
Serves: 2

*You may use 1 medium yellow turnip. This will have a stronger flavor, which is improved by adding 1/2 chicken boullion cube to the water.

SAUTEED WATERCRESS

Cooked watercress may be a first for many people, but it will then become a favorite. It's deliciously different, pretty, and very nourishing.

INGREDIENTS	UTENSILS
1/2 bunch watercress, washed and drained	paring knife
	colander or large strainer
1 tbsp. vegetable oil	mixing spoon
1/8 tsp. white pepper	measuring spoons
1/8 tsp. garlic powder	large, heavy skillet
1/4 tsp. salt	dishpan or large pot

Cut 1/2" off bottom of watercress stems. Soak watercress in cold water. Wash and drain in strainer.

Just before serving, heat oil, salt, pepper, and garlic powder in skillet. When oil is just hot but not smoking, add watercress. Stir over medium heat for 30 seconds.

Time: preparation: 3 minutes
cooking: 1 minute
Serves: 2

BASIC PANNED ZUCCHINI

This basic recipe is so fast and delicious that you will never boil zucchini or summer squash again. Furthermore, it is so versatile a recipe that you can omit the oregano or add any other herb or flavor you favor with similar success. The variations that follow this basic plan are equally easy and delicious.

INGREDIENTS
2 tbsp. butter
1 small onion, peeled and sliced
thin
2 medium zucchini, washed and
sliced about 1/8" thick
1/2 tsp. salt
1/4 tsp. white pepper
1/2 tsp. dried oregano

UTENSILS
large, heavy skillet
with lid
paring knife
cutting board
mixing spoon
measuring spoons

Put butter in skillet and melt over medium heat until bubbly. Slice onion and zucchini; add to skillet along with seasonings. Stir well. Cover and cook slowly 8-10 minutes, stirring occasionally, until zucchini is just tender. Stir and serve.

Time: 10-12 minutes
Serves: 2

CURRIED ZUCCHINI

Use the Basic Panned Zucchini recipe, but omit the oregano and instead add 1½ tsp. curry powder to the melted butter and stir well before adding the vegetables. Time: 10-12 minutes.

CHEDDAR ZUCCHINI

Use the Basic Panned Zucchini recipe. While zucchini is cooking, cut up a 2x2x1" cube of Cheddar cheese with your knife. When zucchini is cooked, add cheese; stir, recover skillet, turn off heat, and let stand 2 minutes. Stir and serve. Time 12-15 minutes.

ZUCCHINI PARMESAN

Use the Basic Panned Zucchini recipe. Organo works very well with Parmesan cheese; but for a variation you might replace the oregano with 1/4 tsp. fresh dill. Whatever the herb, cook as directed. Just before serving, sprinkle 3 tbsp. grated Parmesan (or Swiss) cheese over the top. Stir and serve. Time: 10-12 minutes.

ZUCCHINI MELANGE

This is so incredibly tasty that you may find yourself doubling the recipe and using this dish as a budget-saving, vegetarian entrée several times a week when zucchini is in season. It works this way. After the suggested raw vegetables are almost cooked, throw in any cooked vegetable or diced meat leftovers you have in your refrigerator. Zucchini magnifies the slightest meat flavor and makes it easy to satisfy the requirements of the most avid meat-eater. The more varied the vegetables in color, flavor, and texture, the more interesting this dish. Substitute thyme for oregano; add curry; add Chinese cabbage, Swiss chard, spinach, ruby lettuce, turnip, or kohlrabi. The only limitations are your garden, grocery, or imagination. And if you don't have any cooked rice on hand, start a halved Parsley Rice (see Index) first thing.

INGREDIENTS
2 tbsp. butter
1 small onion, peeled and sliced
   thin
1/2 tsp. salt
1/4 tsp. white pepper
1/2 tsp. oregano
1 stalk celery, sliced thin
3 flowerettes raw cauliflower or
   broccoli, sliced thin
1 carrot, sliced thin
2 medium zucchini*, washed and
   sliced 1/8" thick
2 ripe tomatoes, roughly diced
1/2-1 c. cooked leftover rice
1/2 c. shredded Cheddar or Swiss
   cheese
1/2 c. diced leftover meat,
   optional
cooked leftover vegetables,
   optional

UTENSILS
large, heavy skillet
   with lid
paring knife
cutting board
mixing spoon
measuring spoons
measuring cup
cheese grater

Slice all raw vegetables but zucchini and tomatoes. Put butter in skillet and melt over medium heat until bubbly. Add seasonings and sliced vegetables. Sauté 2 minutes. Meanwhile prepare zucchini and tomatoes and add to pan. Stir, cover, and cook 8-10 minutes, stirring occasionally. Prepare cooked vegetables and meat.

Remove cover and stir in any cooked vegetables or diced cooked meat you want to add, and also the cooked rice. Cover and cook 2 minutes or until all vegetables are hot. Stir occasionally. Shred the cheese and add to skillet. Remove from heat. Stir, cover, and let stand until cheese is melted (about 1 minute). Stir and serve.

Time: 16-20 minutes
Serves: 2 very generously

*The more other vegetables you use, the less zucchini you need.

ZUCCHINI PANCAKES

On the order of potato pancakes but of a different texture and more subtle taste. Surprisingly easy to devour.

INGREDIENTS
1/4 c. Wondra granulated flour
1/2 tsp. salt
1/8 tsp. pepper
1 egg, separated
1 c. shredded, unpeeled zucchini
   (about 6" long)
1/2 c. shredded Cheddar cheese
1 small onion, minced fine
1 tbsp. fresh basil, minced
1 tbsp. fresh parsley, minced
1/4 c. vegetable oil

UTENSILS
large bowl
medium bowl
measuring cup
cutting board
paring knife
measuring spoons
cheese grater
electric beater
fork
large, heavy skillet*
metal spatula
2 paper towels

Measure flour. Stir flour, salt, and pepper into large bowl. Shred zucchini and Cheddar cheese and add to large bowl; mix with fork. Separate egg whites to medium bowl, add egg yolk to large bowl. Mince onion, basil, and parsley, and add to large bowl. Mix large-bowl mixture with fork. Add vegetable oil to skillet over medium-high heat (do not let oil smoke or burn) while you beat egg white until stiff. Add beaten egg white to large bowl and mix gently with fork.

Put 5 or 6 tablespoon blobs in skillet over medium heat and cook for about 4 minutes. Turn pancakes and cook 3 minutes more. Remove cooked pancakes to paper towels. Add remaining mixture to skillet and cook in the same manner. Serve immediately. Makes 10-12 pancakes.

Time: preparation: 10 minutes
        cooking: 7-14 minutes*
Serves: 2 generously

*You could cut the cooking time by 7 minutes by using a griddle and cooking all the pancakes at once.

SALADS and DRESSINGS

See also Index for:

AVOCADO SALAD DRESSING

The fresh creamy texture and definite green color make this a most pleasing dressing. Best served over very crisp lettuces, it is also the perfect accompaniment to a spicy dinner. Can be made several days in advance.

INGREDIENTS
1/2 c. Hellmann's mayonnaise
1/2 c. milk
1/2 avocado, peeled and cut into
  chunks
1 green onion, chopped, or
  2 tbsp. chives, chopped
1/2 tsp. salt
1/4 tsp. freshly ground black
  pepper
1/4 tsp. garlic powder
2 large sprigs fresh parsley
2 tbsp. lemon juice

UTENSILS
measuring cup
measuring spoons
paring knife
blender or food
  processor
cutting board

Measure mayonnaise and milk into blender. Prepare avocado and onion and add with all other ingredients to blender. Cover and blend 1 minute or until smooth. Store covered in refrigerator until ready to serve.

Time: 5 minutes
Makes: 1⅓ cups

DIJON DRESSING

A light, subtle, and most interesting salad dressing. It is especially good on Bibb lettuce. Can be made several days in advance.

INGREDIENTS
2/3 c. vegetable oil
2 tbsp. fresh chives, chopped
2 tsp. sugar
1½ tsp. salt
1/4 tsp. freshly ground black
  pepper
5 tsp. Dijon mustard
3 tbsp. red wine vinegar

UTENSILS
1½-2-c. measuring jar
  with lid
measuring spoons
scissors or paring knife
  and cutting board

Measure oil into jar. Prepare chives. Add chives and all remaining ingredients to jar. Cover and shake until well blended. Refrigerate until ready to serve. Shake well before serving.

Time: 3 minutes
Makes: 1 cup

CREAMY CHEESE DRESSING

An outstanding, mild, delightful cheese dressing that will please even non-cheese lovers. Can be made several days in advance.

INGREDIENTS
1 c. Hellmann's mayonnaise
1/2 c. milk
2 oz. Gruyere cheese, cut in 1/2"
    cubes
1 tbsp. grated Parmesan cheese
1 tsp. salt
1/4 tsp. freshly ground black
    pepper
1 tsp. onion powder
1/4 tsp. garlic powder
1 tsp. celery salt
4 tsp. wine vinegar
1 sprig fresh parsley or
    1 tsp. dried

UTENSILS
measuring spoons
paring knife
blender or food
    processor
2-c. measuring jar
    with lid

Measure mayonnaise and milk into blender. Cube cheese. Put all ingredients into blender. Cover and blend 30-60 seconds or until smooth. Cover and refrigerate until ready to serve.

Time: 5-6 minutes
Makes: approximately 1⅔ cups

CURRY DRESSING

Just the right dressing when you're looking for something speedy, different, and a little bit exotic. Can be made several days in advance.

INGREDIENTS
1/2 c. Hellmann's mayonnaise
2 tsp. lemon juice
1/2 tsp. salt
1 tsp. curry powder dissolved in
    2 tbsp. cold water

UTENSILS
measuring spoons
mixing spoon
1-c. measuring jar
    with lid

Measure mayonnaise into measuring jar. Add all other ingredients and mix well. Store covered in refrigerator until ready to toss with salad.

Time: 2 minutes
Makes: approximately 1/2 cup

VOLGA DRESSING

Quick version of the classic and also an excellent dip.

INGREDIENTS
1/2 c. Hellmann's mayonnaise
1 tbsp. ketchup
1/4 tsp. freshly ground black
    pepper
2 tsp. lemon juice
1 tsp. horseradish
1/2 tsp. prepared mustard
2 green onions, chopped, or
    2 tbsp. chopped chives

UTENSILS
measuring spoons
1-c. measuring jar with
    lid
paring knife
fork
cutting board

Measure mayonnaise into jar. Chop onions. Add onions and all other ingredients to jar. Stir until smooth. Cover and refrigerate until ready to serve.

Time: 4 minutes
Makes: approximately 3/4 cup

GARDEN DRESSING

A colorful sweet-and-sour dressing that is both very healthy and refreshing, as well as different and delicious.

INGREDIENTS
1¼ tsp. salt
1 tbsp. granulated sugar
1/4 tsp. dry mustard
3 tbsp. cider vinegar
2/3 c. olive oil
1 small carrot, peeled
1/2 small yellow onion
2 tbsp. fresh parsley

UTENSILS
food processor or
    blender
measuring spoons
vegetable peeler
paring knife
rubber spatula
1½-c. measuring jar
    with lid

Measure salt, mustard, sugar, and vinegar into food processor. Blend well. Peel carrot. Slice carrot and onion into processor. Blend until smooth. Add parsley and oil. Blend. Pour into jar and refrigerate.

Time   5 minutes
Makes: 1-1¼ cups

GREEN SALAD DRESSING

A creamy, tangy, pretty dressing that is good on almost any salad and will never bore you. Excellent dip. Can be made several days in advance.

INGREDIENTS
1/2 c. Hellmann's mayonnaise
1/2 c. sour cream
8 tsp. lemon juice
1¾ tsp. salt
1 tsp. freshly ground black
  pepper
2 heaping tbsp. chives, chopped
2 heaping tbsp. fresh parsley,
  minced

UTENSILS
measuring spoons
paring knife
1½-2-c. measuring jar
  with lid
cutting board
fork

Prepare chives and parsley. Measure mayonnaise and sour cream into jar. Add all other ingredients and mix well with fork. Cover and refrigerate until ready to use.

Time: 3 minutes
Makes: 1¼ cups

HERB AND GARLIC DRESSING

Fresh herbs are always preferable and 1 heaping tbsp. of any combination of them makes a tasty substitute for the dried tarragon and basil. Can be made several days in advance.

INGREDIENTS
2/3 c. vegetable or olive oil
1 tsp. dry mustard
1 tsp. salt
1/4 tsp. sugar
1/2 tsp. freshly ground black
  pepper
1/4 tsp. garlic powder
1/4 tsp. dried tarragon
1/4 tsp. dried basil
1 tbsp. chives, chopped
1 tbsp. fresh parsley, minced
3 tbsp. red wine vinegar

UTENSILS
measuring spoons
1½-2-c. measuring jar
  with lid
paring knife
cutting board

Prepare chives and parsley. Measure oil into jar. Add all other ingredients. Cover and shake well. Refrigerate until ready to use.

Time: 4 minutes
Makes: approximately 3/4 cup

LEMON BASIL DRESSING

Refreshingly different. Good with any salad green, but at its best on Bibb or redleaf lettuce.

INGREDIENTS
3/4 c. olive oil
1/4 c. fresh lemon juice
1/4 tsp. dried basil
1/4 tsp. onion powder
1/2 tsp. dry mustard
1/2 tsp. sugar
1/2 tsp. salt
1/8 tsp. pepper

UTENSILS
lemon juicer
2-c. measuring jar with
  lid
measuring spoons

Measure olive oil and lemon juice into jar. Add all other ingredients, cover, and shake until blended. Refrigerate until ready to serve. Shake well before serving.

Time: 3 minutes
Makes: 1 cup

LIL'S SALAD DRESSING

A light, snappy dressing that enhances any salad. Can be made several days in advance.

INGREDIENTS
2/3 c. vegetable oil
1 tsp. dry mustard
1 tsp. black pepper
1 tsp. Lowry's seasoned salt
1/4 tsp. salt
1/8 tsp. garlic powder
3 tbsp. tarragon vinegar

UTENSILS
measuring spoons
1½-2-c. measuring jar
  with lid

Measure oil into jar. Add all other ingredients. Cover, shake until well blended, and refrigerate. Shake again before serving.

Time: 2-3 minutes
Makes: approximately 2/3 cup

PEGGY'S CAESAR SALAD DRESSING

This scrumptuous dressing is at its best when served on crisp Romaine lettuce and topped with freshly sautéed croutons (see Index for Parmesan Bread Cubes). Can be made several days in advance.

INGREDIENTS
1 tbsp. lemon juice
4 tsp. red wine vinegar
1 egg yolk
1¼ tsp. salt
1/4 freshly ground black
    pepper
1/8 tsp. cayenne pepper
1/4 tsp. Worcestershire sauce
5 tbsp. freshly grated Parmesan
    cheese or 3 tbsp. packaged,
    grated Parmesan cheese
1/4-1/2 tsp. garlic powder
1/2 c. vegetable oil

UTENSILS
measuring cup
measuring spoons
small wire whisk or
    fork
small bowl or half-
    gallon plastic
    container with lid
cheese grater

Put lemon juice, vinegar, and egg yolk into bowl. Beat with whisk until smooth. Add all remaining ingredients but oil and beat. When ingredients are well blended, slowly beat in the oil until dressing is smooth and creamy. Cover and refrigerate until serving time. Whisk again before serving.

Time: 5-7 minutes
Makes: 2/3 cup

SWEET COLE SLAW

The ingredients are simple, but the taste is sensational.

INGREDIENTS
1 small cabbage or 1/2 large
    cabbage, cored
1/2 c. Hellmann's mayonnaise
3 tbsp. granulated sugar
2 tbsp. white vinegar

UTENSILS
large bowl
large knife
cutting board
measuring cup
measuring spoons
mixing spoon
wire whisk

Put mayonnaise, sugar, and vinegar into bowl and whisk until smooth. Slice cabbage thin. Add to bowl and mix well. Refrigerate for at least 15 minutes.

Time: preparation: 2-5 minutes
        refrigeration: 15 minutes
Serves: 2

SPICY COLE SLAW

You can change this basic cole slaw recipe by adding 2 strips of crumbled, crispy bacon or adding a grated carrot. For a more visually interesting salad, substitute purple cabbage and add 1/4 cup chopped green pepper. This salad improves with age, so you might want to double the recipe just to have some the following evening.

INGREDIENTS
2 c. cabbage (about 1/2 very
    small cabbage), sliced very
    thin
1/3 c. Hellmann's mayonnaise
1 tsp. sugar
1/2 tsp. salt
1/8 tsp. freshly ground pepper
1 green onion, sliced thin, or
    2 tbsp. chopped fresh chives
    or 1/4 tsp. onion powder
2 tsp. lemon juice
1 tbsp. fresh parsley, minced

UTENSILS
measuring cup
measuring spoons
large, sharp knife
cutting board
salad bowl

Remove center of cabbage core; slice cabbage thin. Chop onions and parsley and mix in salad bowl along with remaining ingredients. Add cabbage and mix well. Refrigerate until ready to serve. The cabbage will absorb more of the dressing flavors if allowed to sit at least 15-20 minutes, but it can be served immediately.

Time: preparation: 5-7 minutes
         refrigeration: 0-20 minutes
Serves: 2

MARINATED MUSHROOM SALAD

Surely fresh salad greens, bacon, and marinated fresh mushrooms provide the ultimate salad for mushroom-lovers. Marinated mushrooms can be made a day in advance.

INGREDIENTS
6 small fresh mushrooms
1/4 c. Herb and Garlic Dressing
   (see Index)
1 green onion, sliced thin
1 c. fresh spinach or Swiss chard
4-6 large Romaine leaves
2 strips bacon

UTENSILS
1-c. measuring jar
   with lid
paring knife
2 paper towels
colander or large
   strainer
terry dishtowel
skillet
2 mixing spoons
salad bowl

Measure dressing into cup. Wipe mushrooms clean with a damp paper towel. Slice mushrooms and onions thin; add to dressing. Cover and refrigerate 15-20 minutes or until serving time.

Wash spinach and Romaine. Drain. Remove spinach stems and tear leaves into bite-size pieces. Wrap tightly in terry dishtowel and refrigerate.

Fry bacon and drain on paper towel. At serving time, crumble bacon over salad greens in bowl. Cover with dressing. Toss well and serve.

Time: 25-30 minutes
Serves: 2

CUCUMBER-CARROT SALAD

A refreshingly colorful, crunchy, and tasty salad.

INGREDIENTS
1/4 c. sour cream
1 tbsp. Hellmann's mayonnaise
1 heaping tbsp. fresh chives,
    chopped, or 1/2 tsp. onion
    powder
1/2 tsp. salt
1/8 tsp. freshly ground pepper
1/2 medium cucumber, sliced thin
1 small carrot, peeled and
    sliced thin
2 lettuce leaves, optional

UTENSILS
2-c. measuring pitcher
measuring spoons
mixing spoon
paring knife
vegetable peeler
cutting board

Prepare carrot, cucumber, and chives. Measure sour cream into measuring pitcher. Mix in mayonnaise, chives, salt, and pepper. Add cucumbers and carrots and stir. Chill until ready to serve. Serve on a lettuce leaf or as is.

Time: 5 minutes
Serves: 2

AVOCADO WITH CRUNCHY STUFFING

A delicious and intriguing blend of nutritious ingredients.

INGREDIENTS
1 large ripe avocado
1 green onion, sliced
1/2 c. alfalfa sprouts
1/8 c. toasted almonds or
    walnuts, chopped
1/8 c. golden raisins or 6
    seedless grapes cut into
    halves
1/4 c. Lil's Salad Dressing or
    Dijon Dressing (see Index)
2 large lettuce leaves

UTENSILS
paring knife
cutting board
measuring cup
mixing spoon

Wash avocado. Halve lengthwise and discard pit. Coat each interior with 1 tbsp. dressing. Slice onion. Place each avocado half on a lettuce leaf. Fill each cavity with onions, alfalfa sprouts, nuts, and raisins. Top with remaining dressing and serve.

Time: 5-10 minutes
Serves: 2

SWEET-AND-SOUR WILTED SALAD

Hearty, different, and very delicious, this can also be doubled to make an interesting susbtitute for chef's salad.

INGREDIENTS
1 small head Boston or Bibb
   lettuce or 2 c. spinach
1 egg
3 strips bacon
1 green onion, sliced thin
1 tbsp. water
1 tbsp. red wine vinegar
2 tsp. brown sugar
1/2 tsp. salt
1/4 tsp. freshly ground pepper

UTENSILS
colander or large
   strainer
measuring spoon
paring knife
cutting board
medium skillet with lid
2 mixing spoons
1-qt. saucepan with lid
terry dishtowel
salad bowl
paper towel

Place egg in saucepan. Cover with hot water. Bring to a boil over high heat. Reduce heat to low and cook 12 minutes. Remove from heat and let stand until ready to peel under cold water.

Meanwhile wash greens, remove any large stems, and drain. Wrap in terry towel and refrigerate. Fry bacon in skillet on medium-high heat, turning once. Slice onion. Remove bacon from pan when crisp and drain on paper towel. Add sliced green onion to bacon fat in skillet and sauté until translucent. Add remaining ingredients to skillet and stir until sugar is melted and ingredients are well blended. Cover and remove from heat. Peel and slice egg. Put salad greens into bowl, cover with sliced egg, crumble bacon on top. Pour hot dressing over all and toss. Serve immediately.

Time: 18-20 minutes
Serves: 2

TURKEY SALAD

This salad is very rich and filling—a good luncheon dish to serve to a large number of people when you boil or roast a turkey breast or turkey roll and increase the other ingredients accordingly. Add peas and sliced hard-boiled egg, then top with crumbled bacon if you wish to add other flavors or stretch the amount. Can be made a day in advance.

INGREDIENTS
1/2 c. Hellmann's mayonnaise
3/4 tsp. curry powder
1/8 tsp. freshly ground black
    pepper
1/4 tsp. salt
2 tsp. lemon juice
1 tsp. chopped fresh tarragon or
    1/4 tsp. dried
1 tsp. chopped fresh basil or
    1/4 tsp. dried
1/4 lb. or more chunk of cooked
    turkey, chicken, or ham*
    (about 1-1½ c.), cut into 1/2"
    cubes
1 oz. Cheddar cheese, cut into
    1/4" cubes
1 5" zucchini, cut into 1/8" cubes
1/2 8-oz. can water chestnuts,
    sliced thin
6 lettuce leaves

UTENSILS
1-qt. measuring pitcher
fork
serving spoon
measuring spoons
cutting board
paring knife
plastic wrap
3 paper towels

Prepare herbs. Measure mayonnaise in pitcher; add curry powder, pepper, salt, lemon juice, and minced herbs. Mix well with fork. Cube or slice other ingredients as directed above. Add turkey, cheese, zucchini, and water chestnuts to mayonnaise mixture. Stir well. Cover pitcher with plastic wrap, refrigerate, and allow to sit at least 5 minutes before serving. Wash lettuce, wrap in paper towels, and refrigerate until ready to serve as bed for turkey salad.

Time: preparation: 10 minutes
       standing: 5 minutes
Serves: 2 very generously

*You can buy a chunk of meat at the delicatessen.

APRICOT SALAD

A most tasty fruit salad with its own special dressing.

INGREDIENTS
3 leaves Boston lettuce
2 leaves Romaine lettuce
1 c. watercress sprigs, broken
    into 1" pieces
1 8-oz. can chilled apricot halves,
    drained (but reserve 1½ tbsp.
    syrup for dressing)
1/4 c. shredded coconut

DRESSING
1/4 c. Hellmann's mayonnaise
1 tbsp. sour cream
3 dashes cayenne pepper
1/8 tsp. salt
1/8 tsp. paprika
1/2 tsp. dry mustard dissolved in
    1½ tbsp. reserved apricot
    syrup

UTENSILS
can opener
measuring spoons
measuring cup
mixing spoon
terry dishtowel
2 salad plates

Rinse greens, break into bite-size pieces, wrap in terry towel. Combine all dressing ingredients in measuring cup.

On salad plates arrange bed of greens. Layer apricots and then coconut. Spoon dressing over top and serve.

Time: 10 minutes
Serves: 2

MANDARIN SALAD

Lovely looks, texture, and taste.

INGREDIENTS
8-10 leaves or 1 small head
   Boston or Bibb lettuce
1/2 11-oz. can chilled mandarin
   orange slices, drained
1 tbsp. toasted almonds*

DRESSING
Lil's Salad Dressing or
   Dijon Dressing (see Index)

UTENSILS
colander or large
   strainer
terry dishtowel
can opener
2 mixing spoons
salad bowl

Wash and drain lettuce. Wrap tightly in dishtowel and refrigerate until ready to serve. At serving time, toss lettuce with oranges, almonds, and desired amount of salad dressing.

Time: 8-10 minutes
Serves: 2

*Buy almonds that are already toasted or put almonds in pan in 375° oven for 8-10 minutes.

GRAPEFRUIT SALAD

Springlike colors and a bright perky flavor combine to make a most exciting salad.

INGREDIENTS
6 sprigs watercress
1/4 10-oz. package fresh spinach
5 leaves chicory
1 16-oz. can grapefruit sections,
   drained

DRESSING
Green Salad Dressing or
   Lil's Salad Dressing (see
   Index)

UTENSILS
colander or large
   strainer
terry dishtowel
can opener
salad bowl

Wash greens. Drain. Remove spinach stems and tear all greens into bite-size pieces. Wrap in terry towel and refrigerate. Toss greens and grapefruit with dressing when ready to serve.

Time: 10 minutes
Serves: 2

ENDIVE REMOULADE

Very quick and different. The spicy sauce enhances this often neglected vegetable. For variety, in place of endive try 3-4 sliced hearts of palm or one small grated turnip and carrot.

INGREDIENTS
1 large firm endive
1/4 c. Hellmann's mayonnaise
1/2 tsp. dry mustard dissolved in
    1/2 tbsp. water
1/8 tsp. freshly ground pepper
scant 1/8 tsp. salt
1/4 tsp. lemon juice
2 lettuce leaves

UTENSILS
1-c. measuring jar
measuring spoons
paring knife
fork
1 paper towel

In the jar mix mayonnaise, mustard in water, pepper, salt, and lemon juice with a fork. Cover and refrigerate until ready to serve.

Just before serving, remove any brown outside endive leaves and wash outside of whole endive. Slice 1/2" off bottom and discard. Dry endive and slice 1/8" pieces directly into rémoulade sauce. Stir with fork. Divide mixture and serve immediately on lettuce leaf.

Time: 3-5 minutes
Serves: 2

DESSERTS

BANANA SAUTE WITH LIME AND WHIPPED CREAM

Very different, very rich, and very easy to prepare. Great for a dinner party: increase the quantity and cook the bananas on a griddle.

INGREDIENTS
1/4 c. whipping cream
1/2 tsp. sugar
2 tbsp. butter
2 ripe bananas, peeled, halved
    lengthwise
1/2 fresh lime, halved lengthwise

UTENSILS
1-qt. measuring pitcher
measuring spoon
electric mixer
heavy skillet
paring knife
metal spatula
mixing spoon
2 dessert plates

Measure cream in pitcher, add sugar, and whip until firm peaks are formed. Refrigerate until ready to serve.

Prepare bananas. Melt butter in skillet over medium-high heat and sauté bananas until lightly browned (about 2 minutes on each side). Prepare limes. Remove bananas with spatula and spoon to dessert plates. Serve immediately with a lime slice and a portion of whipped cream on the side of each plate.

To eat this properly, lime should be squeezed over bananas, then bananas dipped bite by bite into whipped cream.

Time: preparation: 4 minutes
        cooking: 4 minutes
Serves: 2

BLUEBERRY-MAPLE SAUCE

Really very nice and very fast. Try doubling the recipe and serving the sauce over pancakes: excellent! Bagged frozen blueberries are a handy item to have on hand. They are easy to measure and work quite well in this recipe even when poured into the pot still frozen. Try pouring them also directly into pancake batter.

INGREDIENTS
1/2 c. frozen blueberries
1/4 c. *pure* maple syrup
1/8 tsp. cinnamon
vanilla ice cream or 2 slices of
    pound or sponge cake

UTENSILS
small saucepan
measuring cup
measuring spoons
mixing spoon

Combine blueberries, *pure* maple syrup, and cinnamon in saucepan over medium-high heat. Bring to a boil. Reduce heat to low, stir, and simmer one minute. Serve hot over ice cream or pound or sponge cake.

Time: 2-3 minutes
Makes: approximately 1/2 cup

APPLE TART CAKE

Very attractive and speedy. The perfect combination of apple tart and apple cake.

INGREDIENTS
1/4 lb. butter at room temperature
(less 2 tbsp., which should be
put into the saucepan for
topping). (Use butter wrapper
to grease baking pan.)
1/3 c. sugar
2/3 c. self-rising flour
3 eggs
2-3 apples, cored, peeled,
quartered, and sliced into
1/8" slices

TOPPING
2 tbsp. butter (from above)
1/4 tsp. nutmeg
1 tsp. cinnamon
2/3 c. sugar

UTENSILS
medium bowl
electric mixer
small saucepan
8" or 9" square baking
pan
measuring cup
measuring spoons
paring knife
sifter
fork
cake tester or toothpick
or knife
rubber spatula

Preheat oven to 350°. Grease and flour baking pan.

In medium bowl beat butter and 1/3 c. sugar. At high speed alternately beat in eggs and sift in flour, beginning and ending with flour. Spread batter in baking pan. Prepare apple slices and overlap them in 3 rows.

In small saucepan melt 2 remaining tbsp. butter. Add nutmeg, cinnamon, and 2/3 c. sugar. Mix with fork. Spread topping evenly over apples with fork. Bake 20 minutes or until cake tester just comes clean. Serve warm. Cover and refrigerate leftover for subsequent nights.

Time: preparation: 10 minutes
        baking: 20 minutes
Serves: 6

BANANA CAKE

Absolutely yummy and a great way to use very ripe bananas.

INGREDIENTS
1/4 lb. butter at room
temperature. (Use butter
wrapper to grease baking
pan.)
2/3 c. sugar
3 eggs

UTENSILS
large mixing bowl
electric mixer
rubber spatula
fork
measuring cup
measuring spoons

2/3 c. self-rising flour
1/4 tsp. vanilla extract
2 very ripe bananas, peeled
1/8 c. confectioner's sugar

sifter
8" or 9" square
    baking pan
cake tester or toothpick
    or knife

Preheat oven to 375°. Grease and flour baking pan.

In large bowl cream butter and sugar. At high speed alternately beat in eggs and sift in flour, beginning and ending with flour. Beat 2 minutes. Mash bananas well against inside of bowl with fork. Add vanilla and beat batter 1 minute. Pour into cake pan and bake 20 minutes or until cake tester just comes out clean. Cook slightly. Sift confectioner's sugar over top before serving. Keeps well covered tightly in refrigerator.

Time: preparation: 10 minutes
        baking: 20 minutes
Serves: 6-8

CARROT CAKE

Nourishing, delicious, and excitingly different. So full-bodied and moist that you won't want a frosting.

INGREDIENTS
1/4 lb. butter at room
    temperature. (Use butter
    wrapper to grease baking
    pan.)
2/3 c. sugar
3 eggs
2/3 c. self-rising flour
1/2 tsp. cinnamon
1/4 tsp. ground nutmeg
2 very large carrots, scrubbed
    but not peeled
1/8 c. confectioner's sugar

UTENSILS
large mixing bowl
electric mixer
rubber spatula
measuring cup
measuring spoons
paring knife
sifter
8" or 9" square baking
    pan
cake tester or
    toothpick or knife
electric blender
cutting board

Preheat oven to 375°. Grease and flour baking pan.

In large bowl cream butter and sugar with mixer. At high speed alternately beat in 2 eggs and sift in flour, beginning and ending with flour. Add cinnamon and nutmeg. Beat 2 minutes.

Put remaining egg into blender. Cut carrots into 1/8" thick slices and add to blender. Grind well. Add carrot mixture to cake batter and beat 1 minute. Pour mixture into cake pan and bake 20 minutes or until cake tester just comes out clean. Cool slightly. Just before serving sift confectioner's sugar over top. Keeps well covered tightly in refrigerator.

Time: preparation: 10 minutes
        baking: 20 minutes
Serves: 6-8

CHOCOLATE CREAM CAKE

Pretty, fast, and yummy.

INGREDIENTS
1 loaf frozen pound cake
   (preferably with chocolate
   swirls in it)
1/4 c. brandy
1 1-oz. semi-sweet chocolate
   square
1 c. whipping cream
3 tbsp. sugar

UTENSILS
serving bowl
1-qt. measuring pitcher
paring knife
mixing spoon
electric mixer
measuring spoons

In serving bowl break cake into bite-size pieces and sprinkle them with brandy. Use the knife to shave half the chocolate square into bowl. Mix gently and set aside.

Measure cream into pitcher and add sugar. Beat until soft peaks form. Combine 2/3 of the whipped cream with cake pieces. Cover top of mixture with remaining whipped cream. Shave remaining portion of chocolate square over top. Refrigerate until ready to serve. Cover and refrigerate leftover for dessert on subsequent nights.

Time: 6-8 minutes
Serves: 6-8

CINDERELLA CAKE

Like Cinderella, something special comes from the mundane. This cake is very moist, healthy, and refreshing—especially on a hot day. And only the very discerning will ever guess that the "icing" is yogurt.

INGREDIENTS
1 loaf frozen pound cake
1 8-oz. container fruit yogurt (not
   Dannon, which is too runny),
   especially peach, apricot,
   blueberry
3 tbsp. sliced almonds

UTENSILS
large, sharp knife
spreader
serving plate

Slice pound cake horizontally into 6 layers. Place bottom slice on serving plate. Ice with yogurt. Repeat process until slices have reformed cake. Spread yogurt on top and sides. Sprinkle almonds on top and refrigerate until ready to serve. Cover and refrigerate leftover for use as subsequent desserts.

Time: 4 minutes
Serves: 8

SUBLIME NUT CAKE

A supremely scrumptuous cake that may well become an obsession with you.

INGREDIENTS
1/2 c. shelled walnuts
1/2 c. almonds
1/2 c. pecans
1/4 lb. butter at room
   temperature. (Use the butter
   wrapper to grease baking
   pan.)
2/3 c. sugar
3 eggs
1/3 c. self-rising flour
1/4 tsp. almond extract
1/8 c. confectioner's sugar

UTENSILS
large mixing bowl
blender or food
   processor
electric mixer
measuring cup
measuring spoons
rubber spatula
sifter
8" or 9" square baking
   pan
cake tester or
   toothpick or knife

Preheat oven to 375°. Grease and flour baking pan. Grind all nuts in blender.
    In large bowl cream butter and sugar. At high speed alternately beat in eggs and sift in flour, beginning and ending with flour. Add almond extract and beat 2 minutes. Mix in nuts with spatula. Pour batter into pan and bake 20 minutes or until cake tester just comes out clean. Cool briefly. Just before serving, sift confectioner's sugar over top. Leftover cake keeps well covered tightly in refrigerator.

Time: preparation: 8 minutes
        baking: 20 minutes
Serves: 6-8

SHERRY-CHOCOLATE LOAF CAKE

You won't believe anything so pretty and delicious could be made this easily. As a variation, drain 1 11-oz. can mandarin oranges and arrange the segments in between the layers and on top.

INGREDIENTS
1 loaf frozen pound cake
1 16½-oz. can ready-to-spread
   dark Dutch chocolate frosting
scant 5 tbsp. dry sherry
3 tbsp. sliced almonds or chopped
   walnuts

UTENSILS
large, sharp knife
spreader
serving plate
measuring spoons

Slice pound cake horizontally into 5 layers. Turn bottom of bottom slice up. Dribble 1 tbsp. sherry over it. Put sherry side down on serving plate. Spread chocolate frosting on top side. Repeat with all layers. Ice top and sides with frosting. Sprinkle nuts on top. Refrigerate until ready to serve. Cover and refrigerate leftover for use as subsequent desserts.

Time: 5 minutes
Serves: 8

ZUCCHINI CAKE

You will absolutely adore this cake, even if you hate zucchini.

INGREDIENTS
1 tbsp. butter
1½ c. Wondra granulated flour
3/4 c. granulated sugar
1/2 tsp. baking powder
1/4 tsp. baking soda
1 tsp. salt
1 tsp. ground cinnamon
1/4 tsp. ground nutmeg
1/2 c. chopped walnuts or pecans
1 c. shredded unpeeled zucchini
   (about 6" long)
1/4 tsp. lemon extract or
   1 tbsp. lemon juice
2 eggs
1/2 c. vegetable oil
1/8 c. confectioner's sugar

UTENSILS
8" or 9" square baking
   pan
large bowl
2-c. measuring pitcher
measuring spoons
wire whisk
rubber spatula
cake tester or toothpick
   or knife
nut chopper
grater
small piece paper towel
fork
sifter

Preheat oven to 350°. Butter and flour baking pan.

In large bowl add flour, sugar, baking soda, baking powder, salt, cinnamon, and nutmeg, and stir well with whisk. Chop nuts and shred zucchini and add to bowl and mix with fork. Measure oil, lemon extract, and eggs into 2-c. pitcher; mix well with whisk and pour over flour-zucchini mixture. Mix with fork and pour into baking pan. Bake 20 minutes or until cake tester just comes out clean. Cool briefly. Sift confectioner's sugar over top and serve. Cake keeps well covered tightly in refrigerator.

Time: preparation: 10 minutes
        baking: 20 minutes
Serves: 6-8

NUT BARK

Homemade candy without fuss or thermometers! Let this be a special treat or a surprise dessert.

INGREDIENTS
1 c. pecans, walnuts, or almonds

UTENSILS
measuring cup

1 tbsp. butter	wooden spoon
1 lb. semi-sweet chocolate	rubber spatula
squares	large, heavy skillet
	baking sheet
	waxed paper

Line baking sheet with waxed paper. Melt butter in skillet over medium heat. Reduce heat to low and add nuts. Sauté 3-4 minutes or until golden brown. Remove pan from heat. Add chocolate, break apart, and stir with wooden spoon until melted—about 2-3 minutes. Spread mixture onto waxed paper with spatula. Freeze for 10 minutes and break into serving pieces. Store extra in refrigerator or freezer.

Time: preparation: 10 minutes
        freezing: 10 minutes
Makes: 1¼ pounds

CINCHY BROWNIES

These brownies are so moist, fast, and superior to all others that you will probably never bother with any other recipe again.

INGREDIENTS	UTENSILS
1/4 lb. butter.(Use butter wrapper to grease baking pan.)	2-qt. saucepan
	fork
2 1-oz. squares unsweetened baking chocolate	rubber spatula
	measuring cup
1 c. sugar	measuring spoons
2 eggs	small wire whisk
1/8 tsp. salt	nut chopper
1/2 c. Wondra granulated flour	8" or 9" square baking
1/2 tsp. vanilla extract (or 1/4 tsp. each orange and vanilla extract)	pan
	cake tester or toothpick or knife
1/2 c. chopped walnuts	

Preheat oven to 350°. Grease and flour baking pan.
    In saucepan start melting butter over medium-high heat. Add chocolate and break up pieces of both chocolate and butter with fork. Stir. Remove from heat when melted. Stir in sugar. While chocolate is cooling a bit, chop the nuts. Beat eggs into chocolate with wire whisk. Whisk in salt, flour, and finally vanilla. Stir in nuts with spatula. Pour into baking pan and bake 20 minutes or until cake tester just comes out clean.

Time: preparation: 10 minutes
        baking: 20 minutes
Makes: 20 brownies

NEW CHOCOLATE CHIP COOKIES

These cookies are the best tasting and most nourishing version of the old classic.

INGREDIENTS
1/4 lb. butter, at room
   temperature. (Use butter
   wrapper to grease cookie
   sheet.)
1/2 c. packed brown sugar
2 eggs
1 tsp. vanilla
1 c. Wondra granulated flour
1/2 tsp. baking soda
1/2 tsp. salt
1 c. quick-cooking oats,
   uncooked
1/2 c. Quaker 100% Natural
   Cereal
6 oz. semi-sweet mini chocolate
   chips

UTENSILS
1-qt. measuring pitcher
measuring spoons
rubber spatula
metal spatula
mixing spoon
large bowl
electric mixer
2 cookie sheets
platter or plate

Preheat oven to 350°. Grease cookie sheets.

   In large bowl cream butter and sugar with electric mixer. Add eggs and vanilla and beat until smooth. Measure flour, baking soda, and salt in measuring pitcher and stir with spoon. Add flour mixture to bowl and mix. Measure oats and cereal in pitcher and mix with spoon; add them along with chocolate chips to bowl and mix with rubber spatula. Put 20 table-spoon-sized blobs on each cookie sheet. Bake 10-12 minutes or until beginning to brown. Remove first batch to platter to cool while the second batch cooks.

Time: preparation: 5-10 minutes
          baking: 20-24 minutes
Makes: 40 cookies

CHOCOLATE-COCONUT COOKIES

A most unusual lacy-looking cookie that becomes everyone's first choice.

INGREDIENTS
2 tbsp. butter
4 1-oz. squares semi-sweet
   chocolate
7 oz. shredded coconut (about 2 c.)
1/4 tsp. vanilla

UTENSILS
medium saucepan
mixing spoon
medium bowl
measuring pitcher
measuring spoons

2 egg whites
1/4 c. sugar

electric mixer
cookie sheet
spatula
fork

Preheat oven to 350°. Grease cookie sheet with 1 tbsp. butter.

Melt remaining tbsp. butter in saucepan over low heat. Add chocolate, break up squares with fork, and stir constantly until melted. Remove from heat, add coconut, and stir well.

Beat egg whites in bowl, adding sugar gradually. When whites are stiff, gently fold in vanilla and chocolate mixture. Drop heaping tablespoon-sized blobs on cookie sheet. Cook 8-10 minutes, but do not let brown. Let each batch cool 3 minutes before removing from pan with spatula.

Time: preparation: 6 minutes
        baking: 19-23 minutes
Makes: 2½ dozen cookies

PUMPKIN COOKIES

Half cookie and half cake, this cookie has a very unusual and deliciously moist texture. If memories of your grandmother's fruitcake have turned you from citron forever, simply leave it out: this spicy cookie can stand on its own.

INGREDIENTS
1¼ c. Wondra granulated flour
1½ tsp. baking powder
1/4 tsp. salt
1/2 tsp. cinnamon
1/4 tsp. ground nutmeg
1/8 tsp. ground cloves
6 tbsp. shortening (margarine
    will do)
1/2 c. brown sugar, packed
1/2 tsp. vanilla
1 egg
1 c. mashed, cooked pumpkin
1/2 c. raisins
1/4 c. chopped citron
1/4 c. chopped nuts

UTENSILS
large bowl
2 cookie sheets
metal spatula
rubber spatula
nut chopper
mixing spoon
measuring spoons
1-qt. measuring pitcher
measuring cup
electric mixer
paper towel

Preheat oven to 400°. Grease cookie sheets with 1 tbsp. shortening.

Measure flour into 1-qt. measuring pitcher; add baking powder, salt, cinnamon, nutmeg, and ground cloves; blend with spoon. Chop nuts.

In large bowl beat shortening, sugar, and vanilla. Beat in 1/3 of the flour mixture, then 1 egg, then 1/3 of the flour mixture, then the pumpkin, and then the remaining flour mixture. Fold in fruits and nuts with rubber spatula. Put tablespoon-sized blobs on cookie sheets. Bake each batch 10 minutes.

Time: preparation: 10 minutes
        baking: 20 minutes
Makes: 3 dozen cookies

APPLE CRUNCH

Crispy texture and a well-loved flavor in the perfect fall dessert.

INGREDIENTS
1/2 c. sugar
1/4 c. Wondra granulated flour
1½ tsp. cinnamon
1/4 tsp. ground nutmeg
5 medium apples, peeled, cored,
    cut into 1/8″ slices
2 tbsp. lemon juice
1 c. Quaker 100% Natural Cereal
2 tbsp. butter
vanilla ice cream

UTENSILS
1½-qt. ovenproof
    casserole with lid
large bowl
measuring cup
measuring spoons
mixing spoon
paring knife
cutting board
paper towel

Preheat oven to 400°. Grease casserole with 1 tbsp. butter.

Mix sugar, flour, cinnamon, and nutmeg in large bowl. Prepare apples and stir into flour mixture. Sprinkle apples with lemon juice and stir again. Add cereal and mix gently. Add apple mixture to casserole and dot top with remaining butter. Bake covered for 15 minutes. Remove cover and bake 5 minutes more.

Serve half the hot casserole topped with ice cream the first night. Cover and refrigerate the remainder. Serve cold on a following night.

Time: preparation: 7 minutes
        baking: 20 minutes
Serves: 4

FRUIT CRUMBLE

A hearty, tasty dessert speedily prepared from ingredients usually kept on hand.

INGREDIENTS
3 tbsp. butter
1/4 c. flour
1½ tbsp. sugar

UTENSILS
1½-qt. flameproof,
    ovenproof casserole
measuring spoons

1/4 tsp. cinnamon

1 21-oz. can pie filling or any
    large can of fruit such as
    apple, peaches, cherries,
    blueberries, etc., in heavy
    syrup

1 tbsp. lemon juice

2 tbsp. brandy or sherry

1/4 c. chopped walnuts

vanilla ice cream

mixing spoon
nut chopper
small bowl

Preheat oven to 350°.

Melt butter in casserole over medium-high heat. Chop nuts. Remove casserole from heat; add sugar, cinnamon, and flour and mix well; remove to bowl. Combine pie filling, lemon juice, and brandy in casserole. Spoon flour mixture over fruit and top with chopped walnuts. Bake 15 minutes. Cool slightly. Top each serving with some ice cream and serve. Cover and refrigerate leftover fruit dessert to serve cold the next night.

Time: preparation: 3-5 minutes
         baking: 15 minutes
Serves: 4-6

LUSCIOUS LEMON PIE

Reminiscent of lemon meringue pie, but infinitely easier to make and every bit as delicious.

INGREDIENTS
1 frozen 9" pie shell, thawed
3 eggs
1 c. sugar
3 tbsp. Wondra granulated flour
3/4 tsp. baking powder
4 tbsp. lemon juice
1/2 tsp. lemon extract

UTENSILS
9" pie plate
medium bowl
fork
measuring cup
measuring spoons

Preheat oven to 400°. Prick bottom and sides of thawed pie shell. Bake shell for 5 minutes in preheated oven.

Meanwhile put eggs into bowl and beat lightly. Add remaining ingredients to bowl and blend well. Pour into pie shell. Lower oven heat to 350° and bake pie for 20 minutes or until center is almost firm. Serve warm or cold. Cover and refrigerate leftover.

Time: preheating and preparation: 10 minutes
         baking: 20 minutes
Serves: 6

MAPLE-WALNUT PIE

This dessert is uniquely delicious and so rich that a little goes a long way. And since the pie keeps quite well, it can culminate quite a few dinners. For a picnic treat, bake in 18 muffin cups for 5-7 minutes. Freezes well.

INGREDIENTS
3 egg whites
3/4 c. brown sugar
3/4 c. walnuts, chopped
3/4 c. graham cracker crumbs
   (8 squares)
1 tsp. baking powder
1 tbsp. maple syrup
1 tbsp. butter
vanilla ice cream or maple walnut
   ice cream or, especially,
   whipped cream

UTENSILS
large bowl
pie plate
nut chopper
electric mixer
measuring spoons
measuring cup
rubber spatula
rolling pin
waxed paper

Preheat oven to 375°. Butter pie plate. Chop nuts. Crush graham crackers between folded waxed paper with rolling pin. Set aside.

Beat egg whites in bowl. Add sugar, maple syrup, and baking powder, while beating until whites form stiff peaks. Fold nuts and graham cracker crumbs into whites with spatula. Pour mixture into pie plate and bake 12-15 minutes. Top with vanilla ice cream, maple walnut ice cream, or whipped cream (1/4 c. whipping cream and 1/2 tsp. sugar makes the whipped topping for 2 portions). Cover and refrigerate leftover for subsequent servings.

Time: preparation: 10 minutes
        baking: 12-15 minutes
Serves: 6-8

CHOCOLATE MOUSSE

A delicious chocolate mousse that requires few ingredients.

INGREDIENTS
1 tbsp. butter
2 1-oz. squares semi-sweet
   chocolate
2 eggs
1/4 c. sugar
1 tbsp. brandy or rum
2 tbsp. nuts, chopped fine

UTENSILS
small saucepan
rubber spatula
fork
electric mixer
measuring cup
4 dessert cups
nut chopper
1 deep bowl or 4-c.
   measuring pitcher

Put butter and chocolate squares in saucepan over medium heat. Break chocolate apart with fork and stir until melted. Remove from heat and stir in brandy. Separate eggs, putting whites into deep bowl and stirring yolks into chocolate. Beat egg whites until frothy, add sugar as you beat them until stiff. Gently fold chocolate mixture into beaten egg whites until thoroughly blended. Put mixture in 4 dessert cups and place in freezer for 20 minutes.* Chop nuts; sprinkle on top of mousse at serving time.

Time: preparation: 7 minutes
        freezing: 20 minutes
Serves: 4

CHOCOLATE-ORANGE MOUSSE

An absolutely scrumptuous mousse that qualifies as the easiest and fastest we have ever made.

INGREDIENTS	UTENSILS
1 tbsp. butter	small saucepan
2 1-oz. squares semi-sweet	fork
chocolate	small plate
2 egg yolks	rubber spatula
4 tsp. granulated sugar	measuring spoons
1 tsp. lemon bits or 1/2 tsp.	1-qt. measuring pitcher
lemon rind	electric mixer
1 tbsp. orange juice	4 very small serving
1/4 c. whipping cream	dishes
	small bowl
	sharp knife

Start melting butter over medium heat in saucepan while you measure cream and 1 tsp. sugar in 1-qt measuring pitcher. Put egg yolks and 1 tbsp. sugar in small bowl. Onto small plate shave 4 crumbly slices off one chocolate square to use later as garnish.

Put chocolate squares in saucepan, break squares up with fork, and stir until melted. Remove from heat and add lemon bits and orange juice. Stir and let stand.

Whip cream until firm peaks are formed. Set aside. Beat egg yolks and sugar 1 minute. Beat chocolate mixture into yolks. Then fold in whipped cream with rubber spatula. Pour mixture into dessert cups and freeze 20 minutes only; transfer mousse to refrigerator section if you aren't quite ready to serve it.* Garnish with chocolate shavings.

Time: preparation: 8-10 minutes
        freezing: 20 minutes
Serves: 4

*If you plan to make this dessert a few hours or a day in advance, you may merely cover and refrigerate instead of freezing.

CHOCOLATE-AND-ORANGE PUDDING

Pudding is too down-to-earth a description of this superbly simple, scrumptuous dessert that pleases every plate and palate. Can be made a day in advance.

INGREDIENTS
1½ c. milk
1 4½-oz. package chocolate
  instant pudding and pie
  filling
1/2 tsp. almond extract
1/2 c. whipping cream
1 tsp. sugar
1 11-oz. can mandarin orange
  segments, drained
1 3-oz. package ladyfingers
1/3 c. sliced almonds

UTENSILS
1-qt. measuring pitcher
medium mixing bowl
medium serving bowl
measuring spoons
electric mixer
rubber spatula
can opener

Measure milk and pour into medium mixing bowl along with pudding mix and almond extract.

Then measure cream in pitcher, add sugar, and beat until stiff peaks are formed.

Blend pudding mixture. Beat 1 minute. Fold in whipped cream with spatula. Fold in drained orange segments.

Line medium serving bowl with half the split row of ladyfingers. Layer half the pudding, then the remaining ladyfingers and remaining pudding. Sprinkle almonds on top. Chill until served. Cover leftover and refrigerate until serving on subsequent nights.

Time: preparation: 10 minutes
        refrigeration: 20 minutes or longer
Serves: 6-8

PINEAPPLE-COCONUT CONCOCTION

More elegant than it sounds and quite delicious. One pint ripe, fresh strawberries may be substituted for the pineapple.

INGREDIENTS
1 c. whipping cream
3 heaping tsp. sugar
1 8¼-oz. can crushed pineapple,
  undrained
1 c. packed shredded coconut
  (4 oz.)
1 3-oz. package ladyfingers, split

UTENSILS
1-qt. measuring pitcher
measuring spoons
electric mixer
medium serving bowl
mixing spoon

Measure cream in pitcher. Add sugar and beat until stiff peaks are formed. Line medium-sized bowl with half the split ladyfingers. Layer crushed pineapple, coconut, and whipped cream. Repeat layering. Smooth whipped cream to edges and refrigerate until ready to serve. Cover leftover and refrigerate until serving on subsequent nights.

Time: 8-10 minutes
Serves: 6

DOUBLE TRIFLE

This is the best trifle we have ever tasted here or in Britain. Out-of-this-world if made a day in advance so that flavors can develop, it can also be served just after preparation. It has become our standard Christmas and New Year's Eve dessert and has never failed to be devoured ecstatically by anyone who has tasted it.

INGREDIENTS
1/2 c. dry sherry
2 packages of ladyfingers or 1 8″ sponge layer cake, broken into bite-size pieces
1 3¾-oz. package instant vanilla pudding
1 c. milk
1 tsp. almond extract
1 17-oz. can apricots, pitted, drained well, broken into bite-size pieces
1 17-oz. jar Royal Anne cherries, drained and pitted
1 17-oz. can purple plums, drained, pitted, and broken into bite-size pieces
1 15-oz. can blueberries, drained well
1 c. whipping cream
2 tbsp. sugar
1/2 c. slivered almonds

UTENSILS
1-qt. measuring pitcher
large plate, platter, or waxed paper
measuring spoons
medium bowl
can opener
electric mixer
rubber spatula
serving bowl

Break ladyfingers into bite-size pieces onto platter and sprinkle with sherry. Drain and prepare fruits. Beat milk, almond extract, and pudding mix in medium bowl until smooth (about 2 minutes).

In serving bowl layer cake, fruits, and pudding mixture 3 times, ending with cake. Measure cream; add sugar to pitcher; whip. Smooth whipped cream over top of cake with rubber spatula. Garnish with almonds. Cover and chill until ready to serve.

Time: 20 minutes
Serves: 8

TART TARTS

This old secret Southern filling is revealed at last. A uniquely rich and lemony dessert.

INGREDIENTS
4 frozen tart shells
1 egg yolk
1/3 c. *superfine* sugar
1 tbsp. butter
1/4 tsp. citric acid,* dissolved in
   1 tsp. boiling water

UTENSILS
cookie sheet
measuring cup
measuring spoons
electric mixer
small mixing bowl
rubber spatula
small saucepan or
   butter melter

Preheat oven to 450°. Bake frozen tart shells according to package directions for 10 minutes, but cut second baking time down to 2 minutes. *Do not let tarts brown.* Remove cooked shells. Turn oven to 500°.

    Meanwhile melt butter. In small mixing bowl beat egg yolk. Add sugar and beat 1 minute. Add dissolved citric acid and blend at medium speed. Slowly add hot butter beating constantly at high speed until well blended. Spoon mixture into tart shells. Bake until top of tart is lightly browned (2-3 minutes). Watch carefully to prevent burning. Serve warm or cold.

Time: 16-18 minutes
Serves: 2

*Finely granulated citric acid may be purchased at the drugstore or at the supermarket under the name of Sour Salt.

BREADS, SAUCES, and DRINKS

BEER BISCUITS

Three minutes of work will yield a scrumptuous cross between a sour-dough biscuit and a yeast roll. Can be made ahead and reheated.

INGREDIENTS
1 c. Bisquick biscuit mix
4 oz. beer
1 tbsp. sugar
1 tbsp. butter

UTENSILS
muffin tin
medium bowl
measuring cup
measuring spoons
mixing spoon
large plate
small piece waxed paper

Preheat oven to 425°.
  Place biscuit mix in bowl. Mix beer and sugar in measuring cup, then add to bowl and blend with spoon. Cover bowl with plate and let rise 10 minutes. Butter 6 cups in the muffin tin. Spoon biscuit mixture into muffin tins and bake 10 minutes.

Time: preparation: 3 minutes
       rising: 10 minutes; baking: 10 minutes
Makes: 6 muffins

CHEESE LOAF

An inviting taste experience: very pretty and very rich.

INGREDIENTS
1 mini French bread loaf (or 1/3
    large loaf)
2 3x2x1" slices Bel Paese or any
    other semi-soft cheese,
    broken into bite-size pieces
2 tbsp. soft butter
1/2 tsp. onion powder
1/4 tsp. dried dill weed
1 tbsp. grated Parmesan cheese

UTENSILS
small bowl
serrated bread knife
spreading knife
measuring spoons
15" piece aluminum foil

Preheat oven to 350°.
  Mix butter, onion powder, dill, and Parmesan well with spreader in small bowl. Meanwhile cut bread almost to bottom in 1" slices. Place loaf in middle of foil. Spread butter mixture on both sides of each slice. Put cheese chunk in each slit. Wrap foil tightly around loaf.* Bake 10 minutes. Open top of foil and bake 5 minutes more. Serve immediately.

Time: preparation: 5 minutes
       baking: 15 minutes
Serves: 2

*Can be made a day in advance to this point.

HERB BREAD

Easy to do and delightful to eat. The herb butter keeps well in quantity when covered and stored in the refrigerator, and is delicious on any kind of toast or potato. Particularly great with salads, this bread is easy to prepare for large numbers of people.

INGREDIENTS
1/2 loaf Italian or French bread
3-4 tbsp. soft butter or margarine
1/8 tsp. freshly ground black
    pepper
scant 1/8 tsp. garlic powder
1 tbsp. grated Parmesan cheese
1 tbsp. fresh parsley, minced
1 tsp. fresh chives, chopped
1 tsp. each fresh oregano, basil,
    or thyme, minced

UTENSILS
serrated bread knife
spreading knife
paring knife
measuring spoons
15" piece aluminum foil
small bowl
cutting board

Preheat oven to 350°. Prepare herbs.

Thoroughly combine butter, pepper, garlic powder, grated cheese, and minced herbs in small bowl. Let stand while you cut the bread into 1" slices; do not cut all the way through the bottom. Spread mixture on both sides of slices. Wrap bread in aluminum foil.* Bake 10 minutes. Open top of foil and bake another 5 minutes. Serve immediately.

Time: preparation: 5 minutes
        baking: 15 minutes
Serves: 2
*Can be made a day in advance to this point.

BUTTERY HERB LOAF

This makes a nice "homemade" loaf of bread for two. This combination of herbs and butter is good on any kind of bread.

INGREDIENTS
5 flaky refrigerator biscuits
2 tbsp. fresh parsley, minced
1 tbsp. fresh chives, chopped
1/2 dried tarragon
2 tbsp. butter

UTENSILS
6x2x3" loaf pan
measuring spoons
small saucepan
paring knife
cutting board

Preheat oven to 375°. Prepare herbs.

Melt butter in saucepan and add herbs. Dip each biscuit into the herb-and-butter mixture until well coated. Stand all biscuits at an angle in the loaf pan (when cooked they expand to fill the pan). Pour any leftover butter over the top of the biscuits. Bake 20 minutes. Serve immediately.

Time: preparation: 5 minutes
        baking: 20 minutes
Serves: 2

PARMESAN BREAD CUBES

The perfect crouton for onion soup; delicious in salads too.

INGREDIENTS
2 slices white bread
2 tbsp. butter
3 tbsp. grated Parmesan cheese

UTENSILS
small skillet
sharp knife
cutting board
measuring spoon
mixing spoon

Melt butter in skillet over medium-high heat, while you cut bread into 1/4"
cubes. Remove skillet from heat. Stir in cheese, then bread cubes. Return
to heat and stir until croutons are browned (approximately 3 minutes).

Time: 5 minutes
Makes: 1/2-3/4 cup, depending upon type of bread used

DOUBLE CORNBREAD

*A very special cornbread that is as delicious as it is fast. Top with chili (see
Index) for a great, and very filling, Mexican-style meal. Reheat or toast left-
overs and serve, as a marvelous change, with butter and pure maple syrup
for breakfast.*

INGREDIENTS
1 8¾-oz. can cream-style corn
1 8½-oz. package corn muffin mix
1 egg
1 tbsp. onion powder
1 tbsp. butter
1 c. Cheddar cheese, shredded

UTENSILS
muffin pan
measuring spoons
mixing spoon
cheese grater
medium bowl
can opener
cake tester or toothpick
    or knife
fork
paper towel

Preheat oven to 350°. Grease muffin pan with butter.
    In bowl mix creamed corn, corn muffin mix, egg, and onion powder
with fork. Grate cheese into bowl and mix with fork. Spoon mixture into
muffin cups, filling them 2/3 full. Bake 15 minutes or until cake tester
comes out clean.

Time: preparation: 6 minutes
      baking: 15 minutes
Makes: 12 muffins

BEARNAISE SAUCE

The easiest, most scrumptuous version of the classic French sauce that we know. It is superb warm or cold with almost any meat. Substitute the cold sauce for butter or mayonnaise in a meat sandwich.

INGREDIENTS
2 egg yolks at room temperature
1/4 tsp. salt
1/8 tsp. pepper
1/4 tsp. dried tarragon
1 sprig fresh parsley
2 tsp. lemon juice
1½ tsp. red wine vinegar
5 tbsp. hot melted butter

UTENSILS
blender or food
  processor/or double
  boiler and wire
  whisk
measuring spoons
small saucepan or
  butter melter
mixing spoon

DIRECTIONS FOR BLENDER VERSION
Melt butter in saucepan over medium heat. Meanwhile place egg yolks, salt, pepper, tarragon, and parsley in blender. Blend on high speed 5 seconds. Add lemon juice and vinegar and blend 10 seconds. Add approximately 1 tsp. of the hot melted butter and blend 10 more seconds. With blender on high speed, slowly add the remaining butter. Turn blender off when all of the butter is incorporated into the sauce. Serve immediately or cover and refrigerate (sauce firms as it chills).

Time: 5 minutes
Makes: 1/2 cup

DIRECTIONS FOR DOUBLE-BOILER VERSION
(This will be thicker and creamier than the blender version.)
Put 1-2" warm water in bottom of double boiler. Place all ingredients except butter in top of double boiler and blend with wire whisk. Melt butter in saucepan. Slowly whisk melted butter into egg mixture. Put double boiler over medium heat and whisk until thickened. Turn off heat and remove top pot. Serve sauce immediately or cover with plastic wrap so that wrap touches the sauce and refrigerate.

Time: 7 minutes
Makes: 1/2 cup

SIMPLE BEARNAISE SAUCE

The one-pot variation of our easy and delicious sauce.

INGREDIENTS
5 tbsp. butter
1/8 tsp. salt
1/8 tsp. cayenne pepper
1 tbsp. water
2 tsp. lemon juice
1 tsp. red wine vinegar
1/4 tsp. dried tarragon
1 tsp. fresh parsley, minced
1 egg yolk at room temperature

UTENSILS
butter melter or
    tiny saucepan
measuring spoons
iced-tea spoon
small dish
paring knife
cutting board

Melt butter in pot over medium-high heat. Mince parsley. Remove pot from heat. Add salt, pepper, water, lemon juice, red wine vinegar, tarragon, and parsley. Stir. Stir in egg yolk. Now follow these cooking instructions closely so that the egg won't scramble and cause the sauce to lump.

Stirring constantly the entire time, return pot to stove over same medium-high heat for 5 seconds; lift pot 1/2" off burner for 10 seconds; repeat this process 3 times or until 1 complete minute has elapsed. Then stirring constantly lift the pot 1" off burner and cook and stir 1½-2 additional minutes, or until sauce is thick and smooth. Remove from heat. Serve immediately.

Time: 7 minutes
Makes: 1/3-1/2 cup

DILL SAUCE

A very tasty dill sauce that uses ingredients that you usually have on hand. Serve with beef fondue or increase the amount to make a dip for vegetables.

INGREDIENTS
3 tbsp. Hellmann's mayonnaise
1/8 tsp. dried dill
1/8 tsp. Worcestershire sauce*

UTENSILS
measuring spoons
small dish or jar
mixing spoon

Combine all ingredients in dish and stir until smooth. Refrigerate until ready to use.

Time: 2 minutes
Makes: approximately 1/4 cup

*For a different taste substitute 1/8 tsp. onion powder.

TANGY FRUIT SAUCE

So simple that it's hard to believe how good it is! Serve with beef fondue, spare ribs, or chicken.

INGREDIENTS
5 tbsp. sweet orange marmalade
3 tbsp. ketchup

UTENSILS
measuring spoons
small bowl or jar
mixing spoon

Combine ingredients in bowl. Stir well. Refrigerate until ready to serve.

Time: 2 minutes
Makes: 1/2 cup

GREEN SAUCE

This delicious herbed mayonnaise makes a delightful topping for cold roast beef or chicken, a subtle sauce for beef fondue, or a tasty spread for meat sandwiches.

INGREDIENTS
1/2 c. Hellmann's mayonnaise
1 small green onion, sliced thin
2 tbsp. fresh spinach or
watercress, chopped fine
2 tbsp. fresh parsley, chopped fine
1 tsp. lemon juice

UTENSILS
1-c. measuring jar
with lid
paring knife
measuring spoons
mixing spoon
cutting board

Prepare greens. Measure mayonnaise into jar and add all other ingredients. Stir until well blended. Cover and store in refrigerator until ready to serve.

Time: 5 minutes
Makes: approximately 2/3 cup

HOLLANDAISE SAUCE

An elegant, delicious sauce that is ready to serve in just minutes. Serve over almost any cooked vegetable, Eggs Benedict, or fish or chicken.

INGREDIENTS
2 egg yolks at room temperature
1/4 tsp. salt
1/8 tsp. cayenne pepper
3½ tsp. lemon juice
5 tbsp. butter

UTENSILS
blender or food
processor/or double
boiler and wire
whisk
measuring spoons
small saucepan or
butter melter
mixing spoon

DIRECTIONS FOR BLENDER VERSION
Melt butter in saucepan over medium heat. Meanwhile place egg yolks, salt, and pepper in blender. Blend on high speed 5 seconds. Add lemon juice and blend 10 seconds. Add approximately 1 tsp. of the hot melted butter to blender and blend 10 seconds more. With blender on high speed, slowly add the remaining butter. Turn blender off when all the butter has been incorporated into the sauce. Serve immediately or cover and refrigerate (sauce firms as it chills).

Time: 5 minutes
Makes: 1/2 cup

DIRECTIONS FOR DOUBLE-BOILER VERSION
(This will be thicker and creamier than the blender version.)
Put 1-2″ warm water in bottom of double boiler. Place all ingredients except butter in top of double boiler and blend with wire whisk. Melt butter in saucepan. Slowly whisk melted butter into egg mixture. Put double boiler over medium heat and whisk until thickened. Turn off heat and remove top pot. Serve sauce immediately or cover with plastic wrap so that wrap touches the sauce and refrigerate.

Time: 7 minutes
Makes: 1/2 cup

ANNE'S HOLLANDAISE SAUCE

No tedious warming of each ingredient; no double boiler. The trick is in the heating: follow directions, and it's really quite easy and very fast. Can be made a day in advance and reheated very carefully.

INGREDIENTS
5 tbsp. butter
2 dashes cayenne pepper
1/8 tsp. salt
1 tbsp. water
1 tbsp. lemon juice
1 egg yolk at room temperature

UTENSILS
butter melter or tiny
    saucepan
measuring spoons
iced-tea spoon
small dish

Melt butter in tiny pot over medium-high heat. Remove pot from heat. Add pepper, salt, water, and lemon juice. Stir. Stir in egg yolk. Now follow these cooking instructions closely, so that egg won't scramble and cause the sauce to lump.

Stirring constantly the entire time, return pot to stove over same medium-high heat for 5 seconds; lift pot 1/2" off burner for 10 seconds; repeat this process 3 times or until 1 complete minute has elapsed. Then stirring constantly lift pot 1" off burner and cook and stir 1½-2 additional minutes, or until sauce is thick and smooth. Remove immediately from heat. Serve.

Time: 6 minutes
Makes: 1/3-1/2 cup

COLD HORSERADISH SAUCE

Goes well with beef fondue, cold roast beef, broccoli, or tomatoes.

INGREDIENTS
1 heaping tbsp. sour cream
1 heaping tbsp. Hellmann's
    mayonnaise
1 tsp. prepared horseradish
1/8 tsp. salt
1/8 tsp. freshly ground
    black pepper

UTENSILS
small bowl or jar
measuring spoons
mixing spoon

Mix all ingredients well in bowl and refrigerate until ready to serve.

Time: 3 minutes
Makes: approximately 1/4 cup

HOT HORSERADISH SAUCE

It is great on hot corned beef and cabbage or Sausages and Sauces (see Index).

INGREDIENTS
1/4 c. sour cream
1 tsp. prepared horseradish
1/8 tsp. salt
1/4 tsp. onion powder
1/8 tsp. cayenne pepper

UTENSILS
measuring spoons
measuring cup
mixing spoon
small saucepan

Combine all ingredients in saucepan and stir over medium heat until smooth and warm. Do not boil or sour cream will curdle.

Time: 6 minutes
Makes: approximately 1/4 cup

ELIE'S MEAT LOAF SAUCE

Everyday ingredients combine to make a fantastic sauce that improves any meat loaf and is delicious in cold sandwiches the next day. Also great on spareribs.

INGREDIENTS
1/4 c. ketchup
3 tbsp. brown sugar
1/4 tsp. nutmeg
1/4 tsp. dry mustard

UTENSILS
measuring cup
measuring spoons
fork

Measure ketchup in cup. Add other ingredients and mix with fork. Spread over meat loaf or spareribs the last 20 minutes of baking.

Time: 1-2 minutes
Makes: 1/3-1/2 cup

RUM PLUM SAUCE

Serve hot with fruit or as a cooking sauce for meat or fowl.

INGREDIENTS
1 7¾-oz. jar Junior baby food
  plums
1/4 tsp. nutmeg
1/2 tsp. lemon bits
1 tsp. lemon juice
1 tbsp. rum or brandy or sherry

UTENSILS
2-c. measuring jar
  with lid
measuring spoons
mixing spoon

Mix all ingredients in jar. Cover and refrigerate until ready to use.

Time: 3 minutes
Makes: 1 cup

NO-FAULT WHITE SAUCE

This classic sauce is included for your convenience. Granulated flour lessens the chance of lumps, but the real secret to a smooth sauce is to stir constantly and vigorously until the sauce is thickened.

INGREDIENTS
3 tbps. butter
2 tbsp. Wondra granulated flour
1/4 tsp. salt
1/8 tsp. freshly ground black
  pepper
2/3-3/4 c. milk

UTENSILS
small saucepan
measuring spoons
mixing spoon
measuring cup
small wire whisk

Place 3 tbsp. butter in saucepan over high heat. Move melting butter blobs thoroughly across bottom of pan with spoon. Immediately add salt, pepper, and flour. Blend with spoon and remove from heat while you measure the milk. Add 2/3 c. milk if sauce is to be used to cream a moist vegetable like spinach or add 3/4 c. milk if sauce is to top a vegetable or meat. Return pan to heat and stir constantly and vigorously with whisk until sauce thickens.

Time: 4 minutes
Makes: approximately 3/4-1 cup

VELOUTE SAUCE

Substitute chicken stock for milk.

MORNAY SAUCE

When sauce is thickened, stir in 1/4 c. grated Swiss cheese and a pinch of nugmeg.

REMOULADE SAUCE

A distinct and pleasing flavor for fish, cold meats, or raw vegetables.

INGREDIENTS
1 c. Hellmann's mayonnaise
2 tsp. dry mustard dissolved in
   2 tbsp. water
1/2 tsp. freshly ground black
   pepper
scant 1/2 tsp. salt
1 tsp. lemon juice

UTENSILS
2-c. measuring jar
   with lid
measuring cup
measuring spoons
fork

Mix all ingredients in jar with fork. Cover and refrigerate until ready to serve.

Time: 3 minutes
Makes: 1¼ cup

TOMATO SALSA

A cinchy, chunky sauce that's full-bodied and obviously homemade.

INGREDIENTS
1 large onion
1 tbsp. butter
1 28-oz. can crushed, peeled
   tomatoes
3/4 tsp. basil
1/2 tsp. oregano
1/2 tsp. garlic powder
1/2 tsp. salt
1/8 tsp. freshly ground pepper
1 tbsp. fresh parsley, minced

UTENSILS
cutting board
paring knife
measuring spoons
heavy 2-qt. saucepan
mixing spoon
can opener

Chop onion coarsely. Melt butter in heavy saucepan. Sauté onion 2-3 minutes. Mince parsley. Add remaining ingredients and stir well. Cook, un-covered, 15-20 minutes over low heat after bringing to boil. Stir occasionally.

Time: 25 minutes
Makes: approximately 3½ cups

FROZEN GRAPEFRUIT DAIQUIRI

Our unique frozen daiquiri is the tastiest and most refreshing one you'll ever try. You may substitute frozen orange juice, limeade, or lemonade for a different taste.

INGREDIENTS	UTENSILS
1 6-oz. can frozen grapefruit-juice concentrate	blender or food processor
6-8 oz. rum	can opener
2 trays ice	

Measure rum into blender; add concentrated grapefruit juice and blend 5-10 seconds. Add ice cubes 3 or 4 at a time blending for a few seconds after each addition. When all the ice cubes have been added, blend only until all ice is crushed but mixture is still frozen. Serve at once.

Time: 4 minutes
Makes: 32 ounces

HOT AND SPICY RUM PUNCH

Serve this superb, warm punch at your next winter party and you'll receive praise not only for its taste—with rum or without—but also for its aroma.

INGREDIENTS	UTENSILS
6-oz. can frozen orange-juice concentrate	4-qt. pot
1⅓ c. dark rum	tea ball or 6" square of cheesecloth*
5½ c. apple cider	measuring spoons
4 lemon slices	measuring cup
2 cinnamon sticks	paring knife
1/2 tsp. whole cloves	can opener
1/2 tsp. whole allspice	cutting board

Prepare lemon slices. Put first 4 ingredients into pot over medium-high heat. Stir. Break cinnamon sticks in half and add to pot. Put cloves and allspice into tea ball. Add spices to pot and stir well. Heat until mixture almost comes to a boil. Reduce heat and simmer 15-20 minutes. (For a more potent drink, do not add rum until the last 5 minutes of simmering time.) If desired, garnish hot punch with slices of lemon and a stick of cinnamon at serving time.

Time: preparation: 3-5 minutes
        cooking: 20-25 minutes
Makes: approximately 2 quarts

*In place of tea ball, take 6" square of cheesecloth. Fill with cloves and allspice. Fold edges toward center and tie with another strip of cheesecloth or string so that spices cannot escape.

MAPLE DAIQUIRI

Simply the best straight daiquiri you'll ever taste—with more depth, smoothness, and subtle deliciousness than the cane-sugar drink ever dreamed of. The secret is, of course, in using pure, premium maple syrup: no simple pancake syrup will do.

INGREDIENTS
1 jigger rum
1 tbsp. lemon juice
1 tbsp. *pure* maple syrup
2 cubes ice, cracked

UTENSILS
jigger (1½ oz.)
1-c. jar with lid or
    cocktail shaker
measuring spoons
ice cracker or large
    spoon

Crack ice. Place all ingredients in jar. Cover tightly and shake hard until mixed well. Pour into glass and serve immediately.

Time: 1 minute
Serves: 1

HOT WHISKEY SOUR

Deliciously perfect for a cold winter evening.

INGREDIENTS
2 Bar-Tender's Whiskey Sour
    mixes
2 jiggers bourbon, rye, or rum
2 jiggers water
juice of 1/2 orange or 1 tsp.
    frozen orange juice
    concentrate
2 orange slices, optional
2 maraschino cherries

UTENSILS
small saucepan
jigger (1½ oz.)
knife
mixing spoon
mugs or heatproof
    glasses
cutting board

Slice orange. Combine first four ingredients in saucepan. Heat until mixture almost comes to a boil. Pour into mugs or heatproof glasses. Garnish with oranges and cherries.

Time: 3 minutes
Serves: 2

SPICY BLOODY MARY

Our yummy drink has more depth and flavor than the standard Bloody Mary.

INGREDIENTS
1 jigger vodka
2 jiggers chilled V-8 vegetable
    juice
scant 1/2 jigger lemon juice
1/4 tsp. prepared horseradish
scant 1/4 tsp. salt
1/8 tsp. pepper
1/4 tsp. Worcestershire sauce
dash of tobasco

UTENSILS
jigger (1½ oz.)
measuring spoons
1-c. jar with lid or
    cocktail shaker

Combine all ingredients in jar. Cover and shake until well blended. Pour over ice cubes and serve.

Time: 2 minutes
Serves: 1

RUSSIAN TEA

Our improved version of a popular favorite is unbelievably refreshing whether hot or cold. Tightly covered, it keeps very well.

INGREDIENTS
3/4 c. Tang instant orange
    breakfast drink
1/2 c. unsweetened instant tea
1/2 c. unsweetened instant tea
    with lemon
1 c. sugar
1 tsp. cinnamon
1 tsp. ground cloves
1/4 tsp. nutmeg

UTENSILS
large bowl
measuring cup
measuring spoons
fork
serving spoon
storage jars

Mix all ingredients with fork in bowl. Pour mixture into air-tight jars.
    To make hot tea: add 1 tbsp. mix per 4 oz. hot water.
    To make iced tea: dissolve 1½ tbsp. mix in 2 oz. boiling water; stir well; add 4 oz. cold water; stir; add ice and fresh mint.

Time: 3 minutes
Makes: approximately 3 cups

FEASTS
and
FACTS

EVERYDAY DINNERS: TWENTY IN 30 MINUTES OR LESS

The numbers beside the dishes denote the order in which recipes should be started, so that the coordinated cooking will produce dinner in 30 minutes or less.

MONDAY	TUESDAY	WEDNESDAY	THURSDAY	FRIDAY
3. Veal Chops Supreme 1. Parsley Rice 2. Broccoli with Lemon Crumbs 4. Blueberry-Maple Sauce over Ice Cream	4. Burgundy Ham 2. Dijon Potatoes 5. Mixed Green Salad 3. Lil's Salad Dressing 1. Carrot Cake	3. Nutty Little Meatballs 1. Noodles 2. Basic Panned Zucchini Carrot Cake (left from Tuesday)	4. Supreme of Chicken with Apples 1. Parsley Rice 3. Creamed Beans 5. Mixed Green Salad Lil's Salad Dressing (left from Tuesday) 2. Chocolate Mousse	1. Sausage and Sauces Carrot Cake (left from Tuesday)
2. Beef Liver Triangles 3. New Potatoes in Sour Cream 4. Spinach Parmesan 1. Banana Cake	1. Southern Cubed Steak 2. Creamy Brussel Sprouts 3. Maple-Ginger Carrots Banana Cake (left from Monday)	4. Sole in Herb Butter 1. Broiled Potato Chips 3. Broccoli with Lemon Crumbs 2. Chocolate-Orange Mousse	2. Sweet-and-Sour Pork 1. Parsley Rice Chocolate-Orange Mousse (left from Wednesday)	1. Tangy Barbecued Chicken 2. Creamed Cabbage 4. Mixed Green Salad 3. Dijon Dressing Banana Cake (left from Monday)
3. Spicy Stir-fry Pork 1. Rice 2. Pineapple-Coconut Concoction	1. Spaghetti à la Carbonara 4. Mixed Green Salad 3. Green Dressing 2. Fruit Crumble	1. Pepper Steak Stroganoff 2. Noodles 3. Mint Peas Pineapple-Coconut Concoction (left from Monday)	1. Mock Coq au Vin 2. Parsley Rice 3. Apricot Salad Fruit Crumble (left from Tuesday)	1. Sneaky Cassoulet 2. Mixed Green Salad Dijon Dressing (left from previous Friday) Fruit Crumble (left from Tuesday)
2. Shrimp Fondue on Toast Points 3. Sautéed Watercress 1. Zucchini Cake	2. Lamb Curry 1. Parsley Rice 4. Mixed Green Salad 3. Creamy Cheese Dressing Zucchini Cake (left from Monday)	1. Almond Fettucine 4. Mixed Green Salad 3. Garden Dressing 2. Chocolate-Coconut Cookies	2. Southern Fried Chicken 1. Broiled Cauliflower 3. Sweet-and-Sour Green Beans Chocolate-Coconut Cookies (left from Wednesday)	3. Shrimp Creole 1. Parsley Rice 2. Sweet Cole Slaw Zucchini Cake (left from Monday)

145

PARTY MENUS FOR ALL OCCASIONS

These are the exceptions to the 30-minute rule—although many of the simple menus will easily fit the time span. Our aim in this section was to provide imaginative menus for a variety of occasions.

Our Ten Formal Dinner Menus are well planned: they appeal to the eye and the palate and bring together a wide range of dishes in successful combinations.

Our 24 Special-Event Menus are appropriate to the occasions and are so easy they should inspire you to entertain more easily and more often.

TEN FORMAL DINNER MENUS

Menu 1	Menu 2	Menu 3	Menu 4	Menu 5
Curry Cocktail Dip with Fresh Vegetables / Sausage Puffs	Curried Crab Dip / Avocado Dip with Fresh Vegetables	Puffed Cheese Spread / Mild Paté Ball	Beef Ball / Onion Squares	Curried Egg Salad / Cheese-and-Chutney Cookies
—	—	—	—	—
Avocado with Crunchy Stuffing	Watercress Vichyssoise	Shrimp and Endive Rémoulade	Tiny Cheese Squares	Carrot Vichyssoise
—	—	—	—	—
Gruyère Veal / Parsley Rice / Fresh Asparagus	Chicken Cutlets Béarnaise / Turnips au Gratin / Broccoli with Lemon Crumbs	Stuffed Chicken Breasts / Tomatoes and Croutons / Creamed Spinach	Fish Fillets Poached in Wine / Fresh Asparagus / Maple-Ginger Carrots	Steak au Poivre / Broiled Cauliflower / Sautéed Watercress
—	—	—	—	—
Mixed Green Salad / Creamy Cheese Dressing	Mixed Green Salad / Green Dressing	Mixed Green Salad / Dijon Dressing	Marinated Mushroom Salad	Caesar Salad
—	—	—	—	—
Double Trifle	Luscious Lemon Pie	Banana Sauté with Lime and Whipped Cream	Sublime Nut Cake	Tart Tarts

Menu 1

- Olive Puffs
- Shrimp Paté
- —
- Blue Endive
- —
- Supreme of Chicken with Ham and Cheese
- Dijon Potatoes
- Braised Brussel Sprouts
- —
- Sweet-and-Sour Wilted Salad
- —
- Chocolate-Orange Mousse

Menu 2

- Black Bean Dip with Tortilla Chips
- Onion Cheese Spread on Celery Chunks
- Asparagus-Cheese Puff
- —
- Scallops à la Newburg
- Patty Shells
- Sautéed Zucchini
- —
- Mandarin Salad
- —
- Carrot Cake

Menu 3

- Shrimp Fondue
- Cheese Cups
- —
- Hearts-of-Palm Rémoulade
- —
- Medallions of Pork with Apples and Béarnaise Sauce
- Beer Biscuits
- Spinach Parmesan
- Mixed Green Salad
- Lil's Salad Dressing
- —
- Nut Bark

Menu 4

- Artichoke Dip with Fresh Snow Peas
- Onion-Stuffed Mushrooms
- —
- Cold Fruit Soup
- —
- Chicken Dijon
- Parsley Rice
- Onions Almondine
- Beets and White Grapes
- Spinach Salad
- Herb-and-Garlic Dressing
- Chocolate Mousse

Menu 5

- Deviled Meatballs
- Cheddar Cheese Ball
- —
- Cream of Spinach Soup
- —
- Shrimp Sauté
- Parsley Rice
- Creamed Beans
- Apricot Salad
- Maple-Walnut Pie

TWENTY-FOUR SPECIAL-EVENT MENUS

Football Picnic

Hot Whiskey Sour
—
Creamed Beef on Toast Points
Raw Three-Vegetable Salad
—
Cinchy Brownies

Touch Football

Spicy Bloody Mary
—
Chili con Carne
Herb Bread
Mixed Green Salad
Green Dressing
—
New Chocolate Chip Cookies

After-the-Hunt Breakfast

Hot Whiskey Sour
—
Sausage-Stuffed Tomatoes
Creamed-Cabbage
—
Zucchini Cake

Christmas Carol Sing

Hot-and-Spicy Rum Punch
(½ with liquor and ½ without)
—
Chocolate-Coconut Cookies
Cinchy Brownies
New Chocolate Chip Cookies
Pumpkin Cookies
Tart Tarts
Sublime Nut Cake

Saturday Skating Supper

Honestly Good Hash
Mixed Green Salad
Dijon Dressing
—
Fruit Crumble with Vanilla Ice Cream

Sledding Luncheon

Hot Zucchini Vichyssoise
Double Cornbread
—
New Chocolate Chip Cookies

Paddle Tennis Brunch

Onion Soup
—
Tortellini Take-off
Green Salad
Garden Dressing
—
Maple-Walnut Pie

Tennis Brunch

Cold Fruit Soup
—
Crustless Quiche au Fromage
Varié
Mixed Green Salad
Dijon Dressing
—
Apple Tart Cake

First-Signs-of-Spring Luncheon

Cheese Cups
—
Pasta Salad
Herb Bread
—
Pineapple-Coconut Concoction

Summer Luncheon

Cold Fruit Soup
—
Turkey Salad
Buttery Herb Loaf
—
Tart Tarts
—
Iced Russian Tea

Vegetarian Feast

Fresh Asparagus
Creamed Carrots
Onions Almondine
Broiled Potato Chips
Curried Celery and Apples
Turnips Lyonnaise
—
Zucchini Cake

4th of July Picnic

Zucchini Vichyssoise
—
Fried Chicken
Curried Egg Salad Sandwiches
Cole Slaw
—
Carrot Cake

Volunteer Luncheon

Frozen Grapefruit Daiquiri
—
Asparagus-Cheese Puff
Mixed Green Salad
 with Curry Dressing
—
Cinderella Cake

Ladies Luncheon

Maple Daiquiri
—
Curried Crab Pie
Mixed Green Salad with Dijon
 Dressing
—
Chocolate-Coconut Cookies

Moving-Day Dinner

Almond Fettucini
Grapefruit Salad
—
Sherry-Chocolate Loaf Cake

Vitamin Vittles

Avocado with Crunchy Stuffing
Herbed Brown Rice
Creamed Onions
Fresh Asparagus
—
Carrot Cake

After-Theater Supper

Ham-and-Cheese Sandwiches
 with Wine Sauce
Mixed Green Salad with
 Herb-and-Garlic Dressing
—
Chocolate Mousse

Midnight Snack

Mushrooms on a Muffin
—
Ice Cream with Maple-Blueberry
 Sauce

Family Supper

Southern Cubed Steak
Bulgar Pilaf
Pizza Peas
—
Mandarin Salad
—
Chocolate Cream Cake

Simple Supper

Lima Bean Soup
Cheese Loaf
Cucumber-Carrot Salad
—
Apple Crunch

Sunday Brunch

Spicy Bloody Mary
—
Eggplant Benedict
Sautéed Watercress
—
Sublime Nut Cake

Poker Night

Sneaky Cassoulet
Sweet Cole Slaw
—
Chocolate-Orange Pudding

Bridge Night

Fondue Meatballs with
 Béarnaise, Fruit, and
 Horseradish Sauces
Cheese Loaf
Marinated Mushroom Salad
—
Luscious Lemon Pie

In-Law Luncheon

Burgandy Ham
Zucchini Pancakes
Creamy Brussel Sprouts
—
Banana Cake

HELPFUL HINTS
Preparation and Storage

PREPARATION

1. Flour. Granulated flour (Wondra) is easily mixed and requires no sifting. Special cake flours, such as Presto, which already have the proper quantities of salt and baking powder, will also save some preparation time.

2. Cornstarch will not tolerate much exposure to wine or vinegar; it soon becomes watery, and the sauce thins. Hence, thicken sauce with cornstarch just before serving.

3. Make your own fresh bread crumbs by grinding bread crusts in your blender or food processor. Then store them in the freezer.

4. Whenever using butter in a dessert recipe, save the wrapper to grease the baking pan.

5. To bring butter quickly to room temperature for use in a cake recipe, put the butter in a bowl, cut it into small pieces, and place the bowl either in the preheating oven for a few minutes (set timer so you don't forget it) *or* set the butter bowl within a larger bowl filled with hot water. For yet another method, follow your microwave directions.

6. To bring an egg yolk quickly to room temperature, break the yolk into a small dish and let stand about 10 minutes near a warm burner or oven *or* submerge whole cold egg (in shell) in pot of hot water and let stand 10 minutes.

7. Whip cream in a 1-qt. measuring pitcher. Why dirty an extra bowl?

8. When recipe calls for a bouquet of herbs in cheesecloth, simply put your herbs in your tea ball or tea infuser. The chain and hook on the tea ball let you attach it to the side of the pot and make removing it clean and easy.

9. To stop curdling of Béarnaise or Hollandaise sauce: remove pot from heat and whisk in 1 tbsp. *cold* water. Reheat very slowly and serve immediately *or*, with blender or food processor on high speed, pour sauce very slowly into machine and then serve immediately.

10. Bone chicken breasts yourself when the breasts are partially frozen. Simmer bones, skin and 2 chicken boullion cubes in water for 1 hour for a lovely stock base for soup or sauce.

11. Try baking meatballs rather than frying or sauteing them for easier clean-up. Cook 1″ meatballs at 400° for approximately 15 minutes.

12. Divide meatloaf mix into muffin tins for individual servings that won't fall apart and are great for a picnic.

STORAGE

1. Save peanut butter jars for storage. Clear glass lets you see your left-overs. Quantity lines on the side make the jar an extra measuring pitcher.

2. When separating eggs, drop whichever part you aren't going to use right away into a small glass jar. Cover and refrigerate. Check our Index for yolk and white recipes.

3. Refrigerate Béarnaise or Hollandaise sauce with plastic wrap touching the sauce to eliminate formation of thick skin on top.

4. Store raw onions and potatoes in the refrigerator. They will last longer, and onions will make you tear less if they've been refrigerated.

5. Fresh ginger has much more flavor than dry. Refrigerate ginger covered with dry sherry in tightly covered jar. Will keep indefinitely.

6. Freezing herbs. Wash and dry herbs thoroughly. Mince and freeze in plastic containers for a prettier color and more subtle taste than dried herbs can possess.

7. Salad greens. Buy a large plastic vegetable crisper to store all your salad greens. Put a paper towel on the bottom and add the salad greens in plastic bags. Remove the greens to wash as you need them. The plastic container will keep the greens fresh longer and protect them from being bruised.

   When you wash lettuce in cold water and drain it, wrap it immediately in a terry dishtowel and refrigerate until serving. Place wrapped-up lettuce in a plastic bag to refrigerate it for one or two days.

8. Parsley and watercress. When you get home from the supermarket, always wash watercress or parsley immediately in cold water. Soak and dunk bunch vigorously (with string or rubber band still around stems) several times in dishpan—changing water often. Line bottom of large glass jar with folded paper towel. When water seems free of sand and dirt, wrap fingers of one hand tightly around bunch while removing string or rubber band with the other hand. Cut 1″ off bottom of stems. Still holding greens, dunk them vigorously again. Shake off excess water and refrigerate bunch, stems down, in the covered glass jar. Greens will keep well at least a week.

9. Bread, ladyfingers, and pound cake all freeze well. If you keep ladyfingers, pound cake, and canned fruit on hand, you can always come up with a last-minute dessert.

MEASUREMENTS, SUBSTITUTIONS, and EQUIVALENTS

MEASUREMENTS
3 teaspoons = 1 tablespoon
4 tablespoons = 1/4 cup
5⅓ tablespoons = 1/3 cup
8 tablespoons = 1/2 cup
10⅔ tablespoons = 2/3 cup
12 tablespoons = 3/4 cup
16 tablespoons = 1 cup
1 jigger = 1½ fluid ounces or 3 tablespoons
1 pound = 16 dry ounces
2 tablespoons = 1 fluid ounce
2 cups = 1 pint
4 cups = 1 quart
4 quarts = 1 gallon
1 quart = 32 fluid ounces
1 liquid pint = 0.473 liter
1 liquid quart = 0.946 liter
1 dry pint = 0.551 liter
1 dry quart = 1.101 liter

SUBSTITUTIONS
1/8 tsp. garlic powder = 1 small garlic clove
1 tsp. onion powder = 2 tsp. minced onion
1 tsp. dried herbs = 1 tbsp. fresh herbs
1 c. self-rising flour = 1 c. all-purpose flour plus 1 tsp. baking powder
    and 1/2 tsp. salt
1 tsp. baking powder = 1/2 tsp. cream of tartar plus 1/4 tsp. soda
1 tbsp. cornstarch or arrowroot = 2 tbsp. all-purpose flour
1 whole egg = 2 egg yolks plus 1 tbsp. water
1 lb. fresh mushrooms = 6 oz. canned mushrooms
1 oz. unsweetened chocolate = 3 tbsp. cocoa plus 1 tbsp. butter
1 c. buttermilk = 1 tbsp. lemon juice or vinegar plus enough milk to
    measure 1 cup

EQUIVALENTS
1 lemon = 2-4 tbsp. lemon juice
1 orange = 6-8 tbsp. orange juice
1/4 lb. nuts = 1 c. ground nuts
1/2 lb. butter = 1 c. butter
1/4 lb. butter = 1/2 c. or 8 tbsp. butter
1 c. shredded cheese = 4 oz. Cheddar-type cheese
1 c. whipping cream = 2 c. whipped cream
1 egg white = 2 tbsp. or 1 oz.
1 c. soft bread crumbs = 2 slices fresh bread
1 c. graham cracker crumbs = approximately 11 crackers
1 lb. flour = 4 c. sifted flour
1 lb. spaghetti = 7 c. cooked spaghetti
1 c. raw noodles = 1½ c. cooked noodles
2 c. cooked cubed chicken = 1/2 lb. raw chicken

INDEX